LINCOLNSHIRE
CATION A
boo'

WITHDRAWN
FOR SALE

AD 03746103

CLASSIFICATION: POETRY

This book is sold under the condition that it shall not, by way of trade or otherwise, be lent, resold, hired out or otherwise circulated without the publisher's prior consent in any form of binding or cover other than that in which it is published and without a similar condition including this condition being imposed on the subsequent purchaser.

A CIP catalogue record for this book is available from the British Library.

Printed and bound in Great Britain.

Cover painting by William Hobson.

This East Midlands edition

ISBN 1-904169-65-1

First published in Great Britain in 2002 by
United Press Ltd
Admail 3735
London
EC1B 1JB
Tel: 0870 240 6190
Fax: 0870 240 6191
ISBN for complete set of volumes
1-904169-66-X
All Rights Reserved

© Copyright contributors 2002

www.upltd.co.uk

A Passion for Poetry

Foreword

Look at life and you can't fail to be dazzled by its sheer complexity. Each person's life can be like a great poem - meaningful, memorable and unique.

But some people prefer to ignore life's complications and meander through their days in a daze. They would rather go through the motions of existence until they realise, too late, that they should have booked a seat on the rollercoaster of life rather than watch it flash by.

If you don't have a passion in your life, you have never lived. Different people choose different passions.

Some choose poetry, and the sheer diversity of the things they write about is clearly illustrated in this book. It brings together a group of poets who can express their passion for life in such a variety of ways.

I hope that in reading these verses you can find words which strike a chord in your heart, and unearth in you a new passion for poetry.

Peter Quinn, Editor.

Contents

The poets who have contributed to this volume are listed below, along with the relevant page upon which their work can be found.

11	Jeannette D'Arcy	36	Carol Underwood
	William Marples	37	Sheila Cato
12	Y M Bramhall		Elaine Marlow
13	Sarah Charlton	38	V Dawson
	John Reid	39	M Ritchie
14	Lydia Dyche	40	Jenny Lynch
15	Polly Taylor	41	Siobhan Brocklehurst
16	Martin Todd	42	Peter Maynard
17	Robert Peckham	43	K J Donaghey
18	Sylvia Rogers		Stephanie Brockhurst
19	Chris Brownsword	44	Hanna Doughty
	Sylvia Spencer		Sharon Hughes
20	Lyndsey May	45	Matthew Cunnington
	Audrey Machon	46	Emma Barnacle
	Grayson	47	Mary Pauline Winter
21	Henk Littlewood		Ben Scanlan
	Melanie Bowler	48	B J Buckley
22	Claire Percival	49	Clara Minichiello
	Lesley Clifford		Dylan Pugh
23	Margaret Jackson	50	C M Harris
24	Douglas Glifford	51	David Hutchinson
25	Pam Summers	52	Julie Hill
26	Lynn Blackwood	53	Jessica Furse
	Sheila Morten		Jean Hamblin
27	Ryan Lambe	54	Kay Jones
	Sandra Benson	55	Andrew Palmer
28	Louise Birkett	56	Lee Busby
	June Feasey		Derick Green
29	Linda Spivey	57	Adam Lowe
30	Susan Mycock		Luke Bramley
	Margret Brooksbank	58	Diana Foord
31	J LeC Smith	59	Nirali Sisodia
32	Garry Knowles	60	Ivan Langham
33	Pamela Booth		Paul Clayton
	Richard Fair	61	Jean Underwood
34	Robert Fitzjohn		Alastair J R Ball
35	Nadia Martelli		

62	Bridget Massey			Patricia Crouter
	Kassia Green	90		Kenneth Chapman
63	Glenise Lee	91		Cath Nelms
64	Mark Allen Gregory	92		Francis McDermott
	Alina Main	93		Elizabeth Chivers
65	Charlotte Thompson	94		Joan Daines
66	Dorothy Blakeman	95		Sarah Clift
	June Fitz Gibbon			E M Wright
67	Keith Powell	96		Lyndis Smith
68	Robin Morgan	97		Caroline Burton
	Maureen Fair	98		James McCarron
69	Margaret Todd			Kathryn Ditcher
	Paul Hughes	99		Linda Stapleton
70	Catherine Armstrong			Shirley Lowater
71	Robert Hunter	100		Beryl Manning
	Mitch Cokien	101		Johnathan Keating
72	Ellen Eley	102		Jennifer Dunkley
	Paddy O'Neill			Ernest Barrett
73	Donald Turner	103		Paul Birkitt
74	Michael Doughty	104		H Charlton
	Les Wiseman			Howard Marshall
75	John Silkstone	105		Gill Doyle
76	Blanche Middleton	106		Daniel Stannard
	Peter Jennings	107		Pia Edwards
77	John Sullivan	108		John Howlett
78	Joanne Brandon			Wendy Holliday
	Patricia Pickworth	109		Amanda Louise Fisher
79	Moonyeen Blakey			Simon Arch
	Sally Chappell	110		William Milligan
80	Jeannie Peck	111		Victoria Ryder
81	Michael Fry			Laura Sutcliffe
	Mary Clark	112		Denise Sampson
82	Amanda Renyard			Joyce Buksh
83	Hayley Nixon	113		Yvonne Bodily
84	Carol Ann Baker			Janet Sheffield
85	Margaret Debnam	114		Michael Lawler
86	Martin Samson			Kym Wheeler
	Paul Russell	115		Elaine Perry
87	Janet Petchey	116		Stuart Griffey
	Sophie Nuttall	117		Michelle Rae
88	Linda Thurling			Duncan Johnstone
	Yuriy Humber	118		Anne Rutherford
89	Jim White	119		Diane Kennedy

	Robert Wright	148	Alan McLane
120	Colin Slater	149	Ian Gray
121	Margaret Whitworth		Corey Martin
122	Paul Wilkins	150	Hazel Walters
	Mary Ricketts	151	Lisa Sapey
123	Jacqui Hancox	152	Charles Baker
	Andrew Martin		Peter Day
124	Beryl Wetherall	153	John Oxley
125	M S Reid	154	Frances Bowman
	Lorraine Diep		Jamie Lee
126	Diana Cockrill	155	L Hunt
	Matthew Williams		Derek Hughes
127	John Davies	156	George Miles
128	Sarah Jones	157	Helen Ambler
129	Katie Li		Heather McKie
	Tim French	158	Howard Hunt
130	Sally Angell	159	Rosemary Rowe
	Laura Walker	160	Nicholas Whitehead
131	Sarah Eden	161	George Shipley
132	Paula Glynn		Vera Bailey
	Juliet Pedersen	162	Julie Mawman
133	Cynthia Fay	163	Maureen Hames
134	Lynn Neal	164	Jack Sadler
135	Elizabeth Morris	165	Ann Carratt
136	Jennifer Stoole	166	Michelle Wragg
	Jacqueline Sammarco		Jonathan Sweet
137	Richard Rochester	167	Elizabeth Roff
138	Shelley Froggatt	168	Hilary Malone
	Elena Uteva		Kirsty Adlard
139	Hilary Cairns	169	Douglas Webb
140	Kirsty Timmins	170	Tracey-Louise Bone
141	Adam Collingburn	171	John Tait
	Arthur Barlow	172	Stanley Chambers
142	Julia Sell	173	Gary Catlin
	Kerry Tasker		Lisa Wallace
143	Stuart Whomsley	174	Julian Cunnington
	David Barratt	175	Simran Panaech
144	Elizabeth Baxter		Kirstin Ferry
145	John Hodges	176	Rosanna Murphy
	Valerie Morgan	177	Elizabeth Draycott
146	John Hopkins		Alan Smith
	Pat Rogers	178	H G Griffiths
147	Pamela Field		Margaret Shortt

179	Norah Hill
180	Peter Simon
181	Maggie Burnside
182	Emma Partridge
183	Stephen Hoo
	Stephen Harris
184	Clare Ambrose
	Lois Burton
185	B Conway
186	Barbara Finlayson
	Sheila Sharpe
187	John Antcliffe
188	Melfyn Dean
	Mary Hubble
189	S Sweet
	P Lipkowitz
190	Leslie Williamson
	Karen Precious
191	C Beniston
	Kathleen Thorpe
192	Stephen Fletcher
	Elizabeth Bigg

TRAVELLING

It's great to travel to places,
near and far away,
It's great to explore unfamiliar territory,
and discover
Diverse cultures,
customs and creeds.
But, the greatest journey of all,
is the journey WITHIN.

Jeannette D'Arcy, Chesterfield, Derbyshire

LOST LOVE

A feeling of despondency, of loss and deep despair
Things that were exciting gone with no one left to share
I offered all of love, for love is all I have to give
That in itself should be enough to conquer all.
I am learning much too late, that love can sour then turn to hate
And make an idiot of man.
What is left in life for me, what can end this misery?
I go through life without a care, like blowing bubbles in the air
They soar and burst, there's nothing left but emptiness.
Someday soon I know I'll find true love to give me peace of mind,
To fill the void to stem the tide; help me, to regain my pride
To lift despair, to walk on air
Then once again my life I'll share.

William Marples, Chesterfield, Derbyshire

THE COTTAGE

I love the village where I live, you can hear the church bells ring,
At night it lights up, you can almost hear the choirboys sing.

You can also see a castle, it looks lovely on a hot and sunny day,
Except when it is foggy, looking haunted, maybe early May.

When it is the kind of weather, like in the month of June,
And you are sat relaxing, after planting all your blooms.

Tensing up when you hear a buzzing, then realise it's some bees,
Then suddenly after working, they fly off towards the trees.

Early evening I look forward to watching the swooping bats,
Then you wonder what broke the silence and notice the cry of cats.

At one, two and up to twelve, the lit up clock strikes on the hour,
It is so wonderful, that a church holds so much power.

I moved here from a town not long ago, the stars are so much brighter,
Living here has given me inspiration, I may become a writer.

Y M Bramhall, Matlock, Derbyshire

To my daughter Kelly Marie, and my son Keiran Ross, for their love and support over the last 16 years.

Born in Gleadless Beighton **Yvonne Marie Bramhall** enjoys cinema, TV, theatre, music, dancing, reading, walking her dogs and shopping with her daughter. "I have written poems for many years on greeting cards, but this is the first poem I have had published," she said. "I would describe my style as romantic and I would like to be remembered as an affectionate, kind, humorous, intelligent, honest and sensitive person as well as a lovely mother to my two children. My ambition is to learn Latin American dancing and I would love to learn to sing and travel to many places." Yvonne has children Kelly Marie and Keiran Ross. "The person I would most like to meet is Richard Gere and if I could be anybody for the day it would be Richard Gere's girlfriend!"

CONFUSED

When doors meet the rain and clocks meet the bees,
And scientific calculators all become trees,
When tick becomes tock,
And purple means board,
And emergency stop changes to sword,
When brushes stir cakes,
And pencils are queen,
What on earth does all of this mean?
When smiles are chairs.
And grass eats the goat,
And how on earth do you swallow a coat?
When drill bits crash together,
Roughly in the sea,
Confused?
You budgie well will be.

Sarah Charlton, Ilkeston, Derbyshire

A LIVING FLAME

The candle burns
Late into the night,
And I sit,
I wonder,
Try to feel what's right.
The flame it seems,
Contains a life,
A hope,
A dream,
An end to strife.
Its light will last,
Till the break of day,
Guiding,
Leading
And lighting the way.

John Reid, Glossop, Derbyshire

SO PRETEND

In our lives
We pretend
Then pretend some more.
Until our thoughts
Are thought to be real,
'Tis then our dreams
Are all we live for
And dream to make them real.

Our thoughts
Become dreams
Then we dream of life,
The way our lives should be.
'Tis then our lives
Become a dream
And so we pretend some more.

Lydia Dyche, Sinfin, Derbyshire

Lydia Dyche said: "I have lived and worked in Derby all my life. I am 33 and first became interested in poetry when I was 15 when I borrowed a book from a local library. The book 'To Be Looked For' by Timothy Island. Two poems in this book, 'Grey Island' and 'To Be Looked For', inspired me to put my feelings down on paper. I am continually inspired by people and places around me, and I hope there is something for all walks of life in my work to inspire them to write."

ME

My dream became the reality of the nightmare
I've lost control over my senses, morals and self
My path to sanity is clouded by my naivety
The lack of interest is what restricts me most.

I'm so petrified of what my future holds
That I'm attempting to live in my past
But my past has been and gone, swallowed
My friends, respect, dignity and knowledge.

I feel like a small child, abandoned by all
Dizzy, confused and lonely as I am I wait
Waiting and waiting for someone to save me
But I know that I am the only one with that power.

But my power is clouded by naivety
And my lack of interest is the cloud of that
Sinking, sliding, crying, dying inside
I smoke the remains of what's broken.

Nothing is left, nothing is said
What's done is done
Just another name.

Polly Taylor, Hope Valley, Derbyshire

NIGHT WATCH

The old world mammal ventures out across the vast terrain
Its snout explores the inner sanctum of an old baked bean can
Rusted ragged edges as killers in the night
A broken milk bottle lies rotting
An empty packet of cigarettes nearby
The old man still coughing
A scent of death crosses the creature's path

This other old world mammal lies torn in the new world
Its crimson seepage stains the worn Tarmac
Here lies the victim of human ingenuity
Rushing
Rushing
Never stopping

The old world mammal now moves on
Its simple life continues
Cautious and curious
Milk bottle
Cigarette packet
Baked bean can
It ventures on as only an old world mammal can.

Martin Todd, Belper, Derbyshire

SAINTS

Saints of old
Saints of new
Life better for all
Sing sing
Open heart
Love in all
All in love
Saints of old
Saints of new
Precious hope
Precious love
Giving all
For God's love.

Robert Peckham, Belper, Derbyshire

Born in Holbrook **Robert Peckham** has interests including natural history and walking. "I started writing song lyrics in 1982 but only recently have I branched out into poetry," he explained. "My work is influenced by love and the natural world and I would like to be remembered as a poet and a naturalist." Aged 46, Robert has an ambition to have more poems and lyrics published. "As well as lyrics for songs I have written about 100 poems," he said. "My biggest fantasy is to travel the world and the person I would most like to meet is David Attenbourgh so that I could share some of his experiences."

GUARD YOUR OPTIONS

I've become a stranger
In this world where I abide
For today I met my Saviour
And I became his bride.

But you see there are no options
When to God men close their eyes
And so we stand and watch
While Satan feeds the world with lies

And he whispers to the gullible
To reap a rich reward
But the portion that he wants of you
You really can't afford

For the price that he is quoting
In his pretensive roll
To Jesus is so precious
Satan's asking for your soul

So open up those options
And feed upon God's word
Just free your soul and heed
The sweetest voice you've ever heard.

Sylvia Rogers, Swadlincote, Derbyshire

MARIGOLD SUNRISE

She is my summer woman
tangled hair of auburn flames
Our ankles clip the ends of a dying sky
as we twist and turn, as we twitch and burn

She is my lady of myth
Keeps the autumn stars from crashing in around our heads
guides me through these funeral nights
as she twists and burns, as she twitches and turns

But then winter crawls in
to start the cycle all over again
dragging her down the shoreline toward mystical light
as I twist and burn, as I twitch and yearn.

Chris Brownsword, Dronfield, Derbyshire

LET IT BE YOU

Clothe yourselves with love, that perfect heavenly gift
So willingly poured out, make sure there's no one left
Who misses out on kindnesses so full and freely given
To counteract this world's bad air of greed and hate and leaven
Make sure it's you who reaches out to put the gentle touch
Amongst those bitter words of strife that hurt and maim so much.
Let it be you to place your hand upon the shoulder bending low;
No one need know just who it is whose tender heart feels for them so.
Just stand aside as they move on, it will have been enough, you'll find,
To let them know that you were there, with empathy so warm and kind.

Sylvia Spencer, Hope Valley, Derbyshire

THE ONE

The night I found you, in walked myself,
Yet a side of me that I'd never known
You sounded like me, loved the same things,
But you were a man with an Irish tone
We sat up for hours and talked about us,
We ate by candlelight, still feeling that buzz
Yet anticipation I felt was not from fear,
As you kissed my lips and held me so near
I knew you before now but we'd never met,
My odds are on certain, if this is a bet
Our souls introduced our flesh and our bones,
And we smiled at each other and said, we are home.

Lyndsey May, Dronfield, Derbyshire

OUR SPECIAL PLACE

Everyone has a special place
Built within their hearts
A special place with love and hope
No one can take apart.

Within this special place we find
A certain inner peace
Where we can turn when we are down
And our troubles are soon released.

We must never take this place for granted
It's with us through thick and thin
Treat it with care
And you will soon become aware
Of the love that comes from within.

Audrey Machon Grayson, Dronfield, Derbyshire

CINDERELLA

Last night I thought I saw your dress
the grey one, I loved you always in,
but in the dark of the bedding
my old shirt waited for the iron's press.
This dawn I wake again distressed,
and yet I set to ironing
that threadbare shirt, its fabric thinning
like me, no amount of carefulness
will steam you out, out of my heart
my head and my hands for a start,
wherein this furrowed brow
intent like the iron's prow
might smooth the wake as you depart
and still eddies in my beating heart.

Henk Littlewood, Bolsover, Derbyshire

OBSESSION

The torture of escapism
Like the torrid flames which burn
Reaches her the possession
Which she had longed to yearn
The subconsciousness of power
In her mind is like a beat
Feeling all its rhythm
Pounding like the heat
His freedom is not within
The grasps which hold his name
For she holds the playing dice
To the motions of his game
She follows his every move
With intensity and aggression
For she's bitten by the desire
Which drives her to obsession

Melanie Bowler, Glossop, Derbyshire

A SMILE

A smile is worth a thousand words that lighten up your face,
It spreads a warmth within you just like a summer's day.
The twinkle in your eye that gleams whenever love's near by,
Is worth the diamond in a ring and the stars in the sky.
A laugh is like some cotton wool, so soft and gentle now.
A kiss is like a silhouette against a sun-filled sky.
This is why I love you and my love shall never die.

Claire Percival, Breaston, Derbyshire

GRANDMA

I guess you knew
That you had to go
But where you went to
Nobody knows

Perhaps to grandad
In heaven above
To find once more
The man that you loved

I miss your face
You calling my name
Because without you
Things won't be the same

I'll remember your voice
I'll remember your touch
And I want you to know
That I miss you so much

Lesley Clifford, Chesterfield, Derbyshire

LOVE BLOSSOMS

Love is a flower
that bursts forth into bloom,
To flourish and blossom
so sweet this rare perfume.

Love is so special
forever in your heart.
Radiating much joy
such beauty to impart.

Love's gentle music
this soothing melody
Richness ever flowing
such peace and harmony.

Love's precious essence
each day grows more profound.
Glorious tomorrows
Which simply do astound.

Love's great enchantment
to share with fine delight
That golden ray of sunshine
forever shining bright.

Margaret Jackson, Swadlincote, Derbyshire

MONEY TO BURN

You bought those nails for your coffin
You took out a passport to die.
You'd tried to give up smoking
Well at least you gave it a try,
At home when you got up each morning
You'd tell yourself a small lie
The coughing's a nervous reaction
And smoking could give you a high.
Now that you're dead and you're buried
You certainly learned how to hack.
You sure failed to heed the warning
Printed on the fag packet back.
You spent lots of cash on your pleasure
You imported the cigs by the sack
You don't know which way you're going
But you surely ain't coming back.
You had money to burn and you burned it
You lived for the day then what's left?
Only stale smoke and a mortgage
And a wife and a family bereft.

Douglas Gifford, Whatstandwell, Derbyshire

THE CHAIR

I love you, dear old chair
Even though you no longer gleam,
Or perhaps, because of that.
To me, you are most special.
It is you who command respect.
Unlike these others, with their vogue, smooth flanks
You were crafted to last, born in dust and sweat
And of curse blasted to apprentice
Feeling this way with plane and saw.
You were my grandfather's favourite
After his long dark days in the pit, he would sit
And chuff on his pipe.
You seemed so ancient, when I was small.
Your arm cradling my back
As I would curl against my mother's breast
While she read and re-read Rupert.
You were the only thing I wanted, afterwards.
Even though your threads lie black and greased.
Just as you are, you are precious.
You hold so much and everything of it matters.

Pam Summers, Ockbrook, Derbyshire

BACK TO NATURE

Islets of copse and hedgerows
Moist grass between my toes
A grassy bank provides my pillow
The limpid brooks runs so slow
Birds provide the sounds of song
Warmth from the sun I've waited for so long
The wildlife take time to stop and stare
Wondering whether I'm alone, or do I care
The trees and bushes provide my food
All helps to lighten my mood
The evening air now slowly cools
The forest canopy give me shelter
It's good to go back to nature

Lynn Blackwood, Swadlincote, Derbyshire

ON TRACING SOLDIERS EIGHTY YEARS ON

My heart aches to see your names
Carved in stone on massive monuments,
Crumbling as all things must.
Eager boys, your lives an involuntary gift
To a nation whose leaders did not love you well enough
To preserve our inheritance.

Some of you lived, your names no less enduring
Inscribed by statute on electors' lists.
Your seed multiplied
And now your children's children
Look back to see the folly,
Look back in wonder

And are proud.
A paradox of perception.

Sheila Morten, High Peak, Derbyshire

UNTITLED

I never knew love was like this until you came along.
Your love took over my soul but it felt so wrong.
We were breaking every rule in the book
But every chance that I took
Was down to you giving me confidence and luck
Because every time I was with you, I couldn't stop believing
It felt as though I was dreaming
I wanted this moment of ours to be strong and true
'Cos I knew I wouldn't get another girl like you.

Ryan Lambe, Chesterfield, Derbyshire

MISSING YOU

I said I wouldn't miss you but I do
I said I wouldn't mind you being far away
But I do
The nights are long without you
Long and lonely, dark and cold
And I lie awake for hours
Missing you.

I know you write me letters
And we speak often on the phone
I tell you that I'm coping;
I say that I'm ok, but I'm
Missing you.

Please hurry home to me and make
My world all right once more
Let's be together once again,
Instead of spending lonely nights with
You missing me, missing you.

Sandra Benson, Oakwood, Derbyshire

BLOOD

Knife flash, swift, sharp pain
Crimson droplets ooze then flow
Spattering the floor.

Louise Birkett, Swadlincote, Derbyshire

THE GRAND MENHIR

I stand alone on empty moor,
Beneath the sun, beneath the moon,
In rain and wind and snow.

The men who raised me long are dead.
Their kingdoms waned to nought
But here I've stood on windswept heath
For twice two thousand years and more.
For what, they ask.
No one alive can tell,
They only guess.

People come and touch, and gaze in awe
And go away across the moor,
But grey and tall, I wait alone.
For what they ask.
I know, but cannot tell.

June Feasey, Eckington, Derbyshire

PEOPLE'S STRENGTH AND COURAGE CAN BE OUR INCENTIVE

I feel so much admiration towards people's courage and determination also faith and inner strength they have too,
With hearts of gold and so much to give with their support and kindness along with natural care in all they do.
People living in a world of darkness having to paint their own pictures putting so much inward colour and true value there,
Whilst those living in a world of silence make their own music doing so with inner beauty, quality and words of care,
To those people sight is only an image and hearing a combination of various noises made,
Because true vision and sound comes from how things are inwardly portrayed holding onto the importance so it will never fade.
It is those who cope so well in difficult situations that deserve all the credit they are due,
And this can be an incentive when feeling so much is beyond me because of what they somehow manage to do.

Linda Spivey, Chesterfield, Derbyshire

A MOTHER'S LOVE

I'd scale the highest mountain,
I'd sail the roughest sea,
I'd batter through, and rescue you,
If you ever needed me.

My love for you is stronger
Than the heaviest metal chain,
It's deeper than an ocean,
More powerful than a train.

A mother's love is special
And not like any other,
One day my child you'll understand
When you become a mother.

Susan Mycock, Buxton, Derbyshire

MY MUMMIE

When my dear mummy died
I really think my daddy cried.
I asked him why she'd gone away.
And if she'd gone so far to stay.
He tried to tell me when she'd gone,
Somewhere high, above the sun
Well why's she gone up there so high?
Did she want to go into the sky?
Daddy bowed and looked so sad,
And said that I must be his good brave lad
But won't she ever tuck me up so tight
And kiss my cheeks again at night?
I think that daddy sometimes misses
Mummy's fond and tender kisses
But then I suppose that one day I
Will too, go up into the sky

Margret Brooksbank, Bakewell, Derbyshire

SPOILED SLEEP

Another night of fantasy
Where errant thoughts obtrude;
An endless chase 'cross endless wastes,
Pursuer, then pursed.

But now I reach the borderland
Twixt fancy and what's sound
And joyfully fling off the shroud
To stand on solid ground.

I pull the tasselled curtain cord
On April day all new
To see the steely starling birds
Pick-pecking in the dew.

To welcome their reality
Simplicity and charm,
And leave behind the troubled night
Of danger and alarm.

Oh pity, pity those poor souls
In lands where angels weep,
Whose waking hours make real the fears
Of my disturbéd sleep.

J LeC Smith, Ockbrook, Derbyshire

WALES SO BEAUTIFUL, I YEARN FOR THEE

The imposing dark mountains all cloaked in fresh snow.
Standing majestic and mysterious with time.
The stream which gently meanders its path.
Anxious to greet the valley below.

The piecing wind through the trees, carries the encapsulating smell.
Of coal dust, and peat on its way
Man-made hills of slag and slate makes this elysium unique.
This paradise, this kingdom I know it so well.

I'd love to return to beautiful Wales.
Where the vivacity is for living and the epoch is timeless
Seasons blend and merge into one.
And the walls of the cottages echo to the sound of Dylan's tales.

Garry Knowles, Riddings, Derbyshire

Born in Alfreton **Garry Knowles** enjoys writing poetry, short stories and novels and also collecting military cap badges. "I started writing poetry at the age of 17 inspired by the work of the poet Marriott Edgar," he said. "I carried on writing poetry throughout my military career, winning second place in a literature competition at St Omer Barracks in 1972." Aged 47, he has an ambition to have one of his novels made into a film. He is married to Margaret and has three children, three stepchildren and three grandchildren. "I have written many poems and have had over 50 published," he said. "I have also written four novels and 14 short stories, four of which have been published."

ROOKS

The rooks are racing now around the trees
Carrying twigs and moss to make their nest
The sunlight comes to play and tease.
Working, fetching, tossing till they rest
New life is stirring, all depression flees.
The sun shines on the snow and all is blest
Despair must go as winter always goes
The darkness of the night
Surely must lift, to brighter lives.

Pamela Booth, Hathersage, Hope Valley, Derbyshire

GO ON DAD

Go on dad, you'll be fine,
I really must be mad,
It's not a fast ride dad,
Go on, it's not that bad.

Go on dad, it's our turn,
I'm not sure that I should,
All the other dads have been on,
And it really does look good.

Go on dad, you're holding up the line,
I feel ill just watching him,
Too late for that now dad,
Here, I'll strap you in.

Go on dad, you can do it,
I'm sure I'll get some stick,
You're the bestest dad,
Just a pity you were sick.

Richard Fair, Glossop, Derbyshire

THE DOOR OPENED

The door opened and he saw
To his great horror, on the floor
Was decay and greenish slime,
And on the walls were dirt and grime
And eerie noises permeating the house.

He closed the door quick as he could,
And then he smelled the rotting wood
As the door disintegrated in front of him.
He saw a shadow, very thin,
Appear in the gloom on an upstairs wall.

His terrified screams filled the air
As he ran so fast away from there.
He heard unearthly laughter coming from the house,
But it just came from the mouse
Who didn't want anyone to live there.

The door opened.

Robert Fitzjohn, Derby, Derbyshire

THE WAITING GAME

One, two, three, four,
hear him opening the door,
five, six, seven, eight,
time to play the game you hate -
don't think, don't feel,
then it just might not be real,
block out the pain,
maybe then you can stay sane.

One, eight, six, four,
hear him whispering for more,
three, nine, two, ten,
time to do it all again,
smile, play, lie, touch,
maybe it won't hurt as much,
eat, breathe, speak, hide,
keep the secret locked inside.

Nadia Martelli, Alvaston, Derby, Derbyshire

NO HOLIDAY THIS YEAR

No flying off to foreign climes, from airports
hidden in fog.
No asking, "Will you watch the house?" or, "Could you feed
the dog?"

No stepping out in sultry heat, when journey's end is
reached.
No lazing by the pool, or drawing lovehearts
on the beach.

No friends, no funds, no energy, no partner,
no one dear.
It's sad to say that there will be
no holiday this year.

Carol Underwood, Bolsover, Derbyshire

Carol Underwood said: "I was born in Derbyshire, where I have spent most of my life. I am divorced, with two daughters and four grandchildren. I enjoy reading, gardening and music. My love of writing and poetry began when I attended Tupton Hall Grammar School near Chesterfield. I have written poetry and prose for several years, and my poetry is based on my own life experiences."

SINGLE BY NATURE

For years I've been a rolling stone
Who wants to gather moss?
I've learnt to blossom on my own
No partner, spouse or boss.
But if I met a special guy
A new leaf I'd turn over
I'd give the married life a try
And with him live in clover.

Sheila Cato, Swadlincote, Derbyshire

COUNTRY LANE

Soft shadows fall
From tall green trees,
Birds sing in tuneful chorus,
Warm sunlight filters in
Amongst colourful wild flowers.

A rabbit hops along
With time to sniff the still clear air,
Frogs croak in the wayside grasses,
Butterflies flit here and there,
Stopping to rest on favourite foliage.

Bees buzz around honey-laden flowers,
Seeking nectar for their bowers,
The cuckoo's call echoes from on high,
From a far distance comes a swift reply,
Nature brings its own delights.

Elaine Marlow, Stanton-by-Bridge, Derbyshire

MY GRUMBLING DAUGHTERS

I love my two daughters so very much
Even though sometimes they send me into touch
Arguing with me about this, that and the other
Arguing too about their younger brother
When will they know of their mother's plight
This person who tries to put everything right
This person who in the night stays awake
And thinks all the time of our lives at stake,
I want to say life's just a gamble
And none of us can afford to grumble

So lets just get on with our loving instead for one day soon we're gonna be dead
It's sad but true we all know that yes
All of our lives lived are just in jest.

V Dawson, Leicester, Leicestershire

Dedicated to the ones I love.

Born in Leicester **Vivien Dawson** enjoys listening to music, walking and all kinds of writing. "I started penning some short stories as a child," she remarked. "Since my husband died I have written a lot of poetry. My work is influenced by animals, children and life in general and my style is thoughtful and caring. I would like to be remembered for my love of life in particular." Aged 55, Vivien works in child care and has four children of her own. "The person I would most like to be is a Victorian lady and the person I would most like to meet is Sophia Loren. I have always admired her Italian beauty and when I was very young I was told that I looked like her," Vivien added.

THE WONDER OF LOVE

I think about you; I love you
I love you; I think about you
You are on my mind; My mind is on you,
I wonder, is there anything else happening in this world-
Except the wonder of what is happening in mine?

There is a hill that must be climbed-
If you want to be on the other side.
You slip, you stumble, want to give up sometimes-
But you are unable to hide.
Go for it you're nearly there-
The summit is in sight
You've done it you've conquered it-
Your soul has heard your plight.

M Ritchie, Whitwick, Leicestershire

AN ANGEL GAVE YOU TO ME

The first time I saw you
My soul shed a tear
My life filled with music
When before I couldn't hear.
A perfect angel, hand-picked by you
Has swept me off my feet
And carried me high on your gentle touch
To a limitless life of dreams.
I smiled as he took my hand,
Let me touch your flawless skin
He said to kiss you
As you held my heart
And wrapped a blanket deep within.
Through my admiration
Our spirits intertwined
And little angel's playfully grinning
As he's left me here with mine.

Jenny Lynch, Ashby-de-la-Zouch, Leicestershire

John, you're my sanity in crazy times and my laughter in tears. I'll always love you. Happy anniversary, Jen.

NEED

As I cry in pain
I shed all my tears,
They fall down like rain
And drown all my fears.

For what is unknown
I know not to be,
I feel so alone
I'm just thinking of me.

I never did think
I could feel this way,
Its not all your fault
That I know what I may.

Discreet is the silence
That's running through me,
No clue what to do
But I want you to see.

I need you right now
To hold me tight,
For I know not
What feels wrong or right.

Siobhan Brocklehurst, Markfield, Leicestershire

JUST A STAR

A star-spangled heaven lies before me,
So near and yet so far,
She hangs by a silvery thread tantalising as she delights the eyes with her flickering brightness,
Greens and blues surrounded by the blackness of empty space,
But it's only empty to our naked eyes,
Really it's full of God's creations,
His hands flung stars into space,
If only I could reach out and draw you near to my heart,
To caress your beauty and survive these aging times,
There is life out there but my eyes are to blind to see,
You look down upon me with a love unknown and yet I am privileged to feel your beauty,
The unknown, the mystery, I cannot explain,
Your stay is not long enough for daylight breaks and your beauty is hidden from my eyes,
But sure enough you will return when darkness surrounds me,
I can look at you once again,
A gift and yet a mystery for all to share.

Peter Maynard, Markfield, Leicestershire

YOUR DELINEATION

The writing is on the wall
The wall is a wall of sound
Some say it starts in the heavens
Some say, it's from the under-ground.

The writing is on the wall
The wall is a wall of sound
It requires your delineation
It requires a couple of pounds.

The writing is on the wall
The wall is a wall of sound
Some say it's the world's biggest mountain
Some say it may never be found.

K J Donaghey, Enderby, Leicestershire

OUR WORLD

This can be a wonderful world.
We all know this is true.
So much beauty everywhere.
Every moment something new.
So why does man think he has the right.
To hurt, to kill to maim.
To spoil so much that God has made.
Fills half the world with shame?
Do they celebrate what they achieve?
While mothers, fathers and children grieve.
Do they really think what they do is right.
That it's heroic to hate and fight?
Can't they see that it's all in vain?
This stupid game they play.
God will return one day.
And take it all away.

Stephanie Brockhurst, Leicester, Leicestershire

I WOULD LIKE TO BE A

I would like to be a bird,
And fly free, in the sky.
I would like to be a dog.
And I'd be loyal, friendly and brave,
I would like to be a horse,
And run, gallop and frolic in the sun.
I would like to be a fish,
And see all of the sea and have no end to my world.
But most of all I would like to be famous,
And sing everywhere

Hanna Doughty, Melton Mowbray, Leicestershire

WHAT A LIFE

Time goes by much too quickly
Things do change all the time,
I wonder what it's going to be like,
When I am dead and gone.

Changing faces, people new,
What are they thinking?
I can remember time gone by,
Different things to see and do.

There's no need to stand and sigh,
Get up and get started,
There's no time to waste on why,
Use the time you have wisely.

Life is what you make it, they say,
But make it what you will says I,
The person who knows what's what,
Is you, him, her and I.

Sharon Hughes, Melton Mowbray, Leicestershire

WINTER

Bare trees move no more,
Snow glistens upon the floor,
Christmas is coming our way,
All the children shout hooray.

Shining ice does not melt,
And the frosty wind can be felt,
Kids with sledges play in the snow,
And the north wind does blow blow blow.

Matthew Cunnington, Cossington, Leicestershire

Born in Leicestershire **Matthew Cunnington** enjoys model-making, fishing and playing the guitar. "I started writing poetry around three years ago at school," he pointed out. "My work is influenced by everything around me and I would like to be remembered as a kind, friendly caring person with a good sense of humour and lots of friends." Aged 14, Matthew has an ambition to become a veterinary surgeon. "The person I would most like to meet is Dave Grohl, the lead singer and guitarist from the rock group, Foo Fighters," he said. "My biggest fantasy is to meet Kurt Cobain, the late lead singer and guitarist of Nirvana."

OLD DALBY DAY

The event which takes place every year,
It brings fun and laughter (and the beer)
Bric-a-brac, cakes, books and toys,
Things sold for the girls and boys,
Eleven o'clock the fancy dress parade,
Children wearing clothes that their parents made.
After that it's loads of fun,
It get even better when the band comes on.
Big Kahuna is their name
Singing old and modern music is their game.
Some people have too much to drink,
While others stand over the village hall sink,
Everything's over by Tuesday morning,
Nothing left but to take down the bunting.

Emma Barnacle, Melton Mowbray, Leicestershire

Emma Barnacle was born in Melton Mowbray and enjoys playing the piano and writing. "I started writing poetry when I was ten," she pointed out. "I like to express my feelings through poetry and I find it interesting. My work is influenced by things around me, films and music and I would describe my style as creative. I would like to be remembered as a happy and caring individual." Aged 14, Emma has an ambition to be successful as a poet. "The person I would most like to meet is David Beckham because he helps a lot of sick people and does hard work for charities," she said. "I have written short stories and poems and had two poems published so far."

LOVE IS

Love is light heart;
Joy is bright heart;
Sorrow is heavy heart;
Peace is content heart;

Hate is black cloud;
Pain is cry loud;
Hope is God's shroud
Enfolding us.

God is love
God is joy
God is peace
God is hope at all times.

Mary Pauline Winter, Market Harborough, Leicestershire

MY CRUSH

I have these feelings, deep inside
Feelings that I have to hide
I don't know if she feels that way too
And I don't know what to do
When we're together, I feel so uptight
When she's around I feel so right
I dream about what we can do
And all the things that we can pursue
I yearn just to feel her touch
And when she leaves, I miss her so much
I want to feel her lips against mine
And feel our bodies intertwine
So for now I'll love her from afar
One day I'll express how special you are
So until then I'll retain this rush
And until then I'll contain my crush.

Ben Scanlan, Loughborough, Leicestershire

SIGHT

I did not walk beside the sea,
Because you see I cannot see,
But my true love who stayed by me,
Said "You don't have to see the sea
Just listen to the birds above,
And to the sounds that you still love,
The rippling waves upon the shore,
Imagine all those things and more."
I walk once more beside the sea,
I care not that I cannot see,
Because my love does walk with me,
Beside the sea I cannot see.

B J Buckley, Melton Mowbray, Leicestershire

Born in Nottingham **Brian Buckley** enjoys writing, music and cooking. "I started writing children's stories and poems when my grandchildren were young," he explained. "My style is varied and I would like to be remembered as a noted writer." Aged 66, he is retired and married to Betty. They have three children. "I have written seven novels as well as children's stories and over 300 poems," he said. "The person I would most like to meet is President George Bush because he is a man determined to bring peace to the world."

MY FIRST EVER DATE

Sitting on the banks of the River Malone
Me and my boyfriend sitting alone
Would I haven spoken? He would not understand,
He was listening to his Walkman

Sitting on the top of the mountain peak
Me and my girlfriend look down at the creek,
Would I have touched her? She would not react,
She was already retracing our track.

Clara Minichiello, Market Harborough, Leicestershire

CHARITY DONATION

He ruthlessly roots out and throws
the monsters hiding at the back:
jackets with six mile wide lapels
and ties by Jackson Pollock.

The trousers where the legs expand
into estuaries, and those
which thin like water in the sand;
the winkle-picker shoes.

He feels good, giving these away
for those whose poverty decides
they wear the modes of yesterday,
those whose least concern is pride,

in how they look. He tries to stuff
back in the wardrobe of his brain
thoughts of the lapse of years, and belts
which will never meet again.

Dylan Pugh, Melton Mowbray, Leicestershire

AND THE CHILD CRIED

Looking through the hurt and pain
Another war and no one to blame
A man lies bleeding, a crimson tide cascades
Like a river to a sea
All this anguish and death means nothing to me
But far away, a child cries

Fear and hate, the devil's henchmen
Stand and survey death and destruction
Where is the hope, love and realisation?
The power of prayer all but forgotten
The beauty of youth an age of innocence
The light snuffed out without recompense

Tears of sadness, a world in mourning
Is man so beguiled not to heed this warning?
A star shines bright in the moonlit sky
A weight is lifted, an end to sorrow
Can there be hope for the new tomorrow?
God sighs, looking down, wiping tears aside
And far away, in a stable, a child cried.

C M Harris, Market Harborough, Leicestershire

Dedicated to Lisa. I love you, always have, always will. Thank you.

NICE IN THEORY

To think we all get what we want,
And the future is all good and cheery,
Always complete and never a nearly,
It's all very nice in theory.

The thought that true love is always,
And that love will conquer all,
It's a lovely thought, a good idea
Very nice in theory.

When you say we'll always be together,
No matter what happens around,
Do you think it truly or are you hiding,
Behind a nice theory?

If you're rejecting reality,
Leaving your dreams here on earth,
Spare a thought for the others, who live in reality,
The ones that can't live in theory.

So when reality grips you
Face up to it bravely
Just because it was wrong
Don't forget a lovely theory.

David Hutchinson, Shepshed, Leicestershire

IT'S GOOD TO BE ALIVE

As time passes by the faces still show the spirit of love.
As the wind still blows and the birds still fly in the air,
there ascends a dove. The rose flowered the day bloomed.

The leaves wilted the darkness loomed, the flower
died but there was a new lease of life. The soil prepared
there was no season.

Cold and icy is the weather cold and icy is the day, I saw
and long for the sunnier times, and dream along the way.
Robins are flying among the trees, and sitting on frosty
boughs.
Church bells peal across the air while people take their
vows. Tall and elegant are the spires loud and wonderful
are the choirs, large and loud is the organ in play, sunny
and cheerful is the world today.

Tall and pretty looked the flowers, whilst I wiled away the
hours, looking for beauty hidden within, the big large bells
toll and ring, the big bright moon shines down below and
the congregation quietly go.

Julie Hill, Harborough, Leicestershire

*Dedicated to my loving mother and father, William and
Eileen Hill, and Bernard, Mary and Christina. All my love.*

OUR WORLD

A falling star, a fairy dream
A world of queries, babies' cries
I want it more than I can dream
But no one listens to my scream.

A million stars to babies' eyes,
A grown man's wail to a blade of grass
I need to wipe the tears away
Solve the pain of yesterday.

Jessica Furse, Loughborough, Leicestershire

SHOULD I TELL?

I've banged my knee,
Knocked my head,
Fell over the toys,
Should have picked them up.
Mum kissed it better,
Clumsy, that's what I am.

The covers are all wet,
Must have spilt a drink I had
Just before I went to bed,
Mum says "never mind,"
And pats me on the head,
Silly, that's what I am.

My friend has bumps and bruises
But she has more than me,
I asked her what she had done,
But she didn't want to say
I told my mum and she hugged me tight,
Lucky, that's what I am!

Jean Hamblin, Leicester, Leicestershire

SUNDAYS

Sabbath streets of childhood
Rang with a softer sound
Nothing sharp or shiny clashing
No one rushing, no one dashing
No clanging timpani of tills
Sundays cured the six days' ills.

Only mother's carving knife
Set up a small affray
Beef or lamb or pork (and dripping)
Sitting in the Swan for sipping
After digging hard all morning
Dads must heed the workers' warning.

Apple pies with custard pouring
Snoozing afternoons (no snoring)
No playing out or having fun
Knitting, sewing can't be done.
Doesn't matter if you're bored
Pointed needles hurt the Lord.

Evensong for winter evenings
Meadows in the summer time
Families fraternising, talking
Families exercising, walking
Over fields of daisied bliss
Knowing God had made all this.

Kay Jones, Kibworth Beauchamp, Leicestershire

SOME GIRLS I HAVE KNOWN BEFORE

Of all council officers, my favourite is Ruth,
Oozing wisdom which belies her innocence of youth?
That sparkling efficient manner pleases:-
So entrancing, its momentum breezes,
In harmonious accord with respect for the truth!

Ms M boasts of having an admired hourglass figure.
So whatever's happened to her pedantic rigour?
Not exactly sixty minutes each way,
But eighty and forty; oh what dismay-
The blubber below the waist is by far the bigger!

Esther's the salt of the earth, not organic acid:
An ebullient character, yet calm and placid.
Though on consideration of her looks;
Rendering me impaled on tenterhooks,
Makes a large part of me the opposite of flaccid!

As the song proclaimed, oh Carol! I am but a fool...
Thereof pondering now about returning to school,
I'm like a puppet dangling on her string,
Yet this bad penny just keeps returning!
If only she'd time, we'd be closely matched as a rule.

Andrew Palmer, Great Glen, Leicestershire

Andrew Palmer said: "Having suffered severe depression and now hypomania, I started writing early in 2002 purely as an experiment and found the discipline of verse a great antidote to my tendency to be verbose. Now I can express myself in a way which gives me great satisfaction and has also made a difference to many others. Women stimulate my creative juices and I have written anything deemed from 'disgusting' to 'lovely' in poetry about them. My fellow villager, Englebert Humperdink is the 'King of Romance' but (with any luck) I'll be giving him some competition for this title!"

THE TRIUMPH OF TWO

The triumph of two over many is a glorious thing
It filled their hearts with joy
And their problems seemed less meaningful
Shouting and celebration rolled off their lips
With beer in their gullets and on their tongues
Hurrah was the call into the bleak wet night
Champions are we two and notoriety is ours
One cog could not turn without the other
Mighty are the few
And few are the mighty

Lee Busby, Leicester, Leicestershire

SHINGLES ON THE SHORE

The sea lies calm tonight
The tide is full,
And fair doth stand the moon,
The cliffs, they stand
So vast and tall.
Across the tranquil bay
The moon-washed sea
Doth meet the land
With gentle cadence slow.
That brings the sadness in.

Once there was a sea of faith
So full and round the shore,
Like folds therein a girdle bright.
The sound now moving in the air
Is a withdrawing roar,
The night wind's retreating breath
Naked shingles on the shore.

Derick Green, Glenfield, Leicestershire

VALENTINE'S DAY

My letter box is empty
But yours will not be so.
I have put aside my pride
To stop you feeling low.
And you won't have to lie
When to see your friends you go,
About what you have received,
If they demand it, you can show
Proof that you are loved
That comes wrapped up with a bow.
Because of what you did for me
In the Latin "Quid pro quo."

Adam Lowe, Loughborough, Leicestershire

WALKING THE EDGE OF THE QUARRY

The wide open Vale at its birth
Nature stretches through groves of bluebells and clover,
Reaching an horizon of grass and clouds
Up the slope through the twisted oak,
We run, careless to the sign 'keep away fools'
The wind so fresh our knuckles glow.
Standing on an edge that seems about to crumble
You hold my hand in total trust,
Walking the edge of the quarry
As the vast bite of it opens below us,
Sweeping downwards one shredded tumble
To the strange machines like Tonkas below
And green woollen moss beside stagnant pools,
The final dredges in the workman's moat.
We scream and our echo returns just as loud
Bounding round the falling cliffs like a lover,
Careless to the threatening avalanche of earth.

Luke Bramley, Ashby-de-la-Zouch, Leicestershire

RURAL ANXIETY

In two thousand and one there was a disease
Which brought our farmers to their knees.
It rapidly spread from north to south;
The name of this scourge was foot and mouth.

Livestock numbers were greatly depleted,
As culling of contacts was completed.
It was a most appalling sight
As livelihoods vanished overnight.

Burial sites were excavated;
Thousands of sheep were duly cremated.
Cloven-hoofed stock became infected;
Cattle abroad would have been injected.

Standstill orders, footpaths closed;
Farms disinfected, vehicles hosed.
Spread is too easy, by wind or a bird;
But it's blown over now, or so we've heard.

Diana Foord, Melton Mowbray, Leicestershire

Diana Foord said: "I am a farmer's daughter, closely associated with the countryside. Having attended an agricultural college, I was a farming instructress at an approved school for Girls in Wiltshire, followed by over ten years at the former Grassland Research Institute. I married a herdsman and happily gave up my career to raise our three children. I have been writing simple poetry since my school days; friends have urged me to 'get published'. Other activities include bellringing, gardening, painting and music."

THEORY OF LOVE

My heart is locked,
Someone is the key,
The person who unlocks my heart,
Has my true feelings,
That of my love,
Goes through the bottom of my heart.
It is deeper than the deepest ocean,
My love for one is hotter that fire.

Love is red,
It is redder than anyone's blood,
Whoever unlocks my heart,
Is like gravity,
Pulling me down to earth,
As my head was in the clouds,
In a dream world.
Thinking,
Who is my true love?
But my true love found me,
My love,
Acting as gravity.

Nirali Sisodia, Leicester, Leicestershire

PROMISE

Stress stress just do your best
I'm four-square right beside you.
All I have to give is yours
Just thought that I'd remind you.

Ivan Langham, Leicester, Leicestershire

FRIENDSHIP

Turn to a friend when in need
Having given favours in the past
Then accept those weak excuses
If friendship is to last

A friend in need is a friend indeed
When they call upon your door
Reward their smiles with giving
They will return for more

The building blocks of friendship
Are weak and always crumble
And the bigger structure that you build
The further it will tumble

Familiarity breeds contempt
Especially with a friend
One constant truth of friendship
Is, that friendship always ends

To hell with friends who have let me down
For them I have no time
We die alone, just as we are born
And that suits me just fine

Paul Clayton, Leicester, Leicestershire

LENT

I felt lost in a wilderness one year
the way uncertain, till God made it clear;
it became a journey filled with trial and error
seeming as if it would go on forever.
I'll never forget it, it made me aware
that God was with me, He'd always care.
To others who might have had a similar sadness
I'll tell them, I now have a heart filled with gladness,
and not to worry, He'll help you through
give life a new meaning, to me and to you.

Jean Underwood, Oadby, Leicester, Leicestershire

Dedicated to my family, family friends and church family who all helped me through that journey.

WHICH ONE ARE YOU?

Which one are you,
Who came in the night,
At the sound of shouting?

Which one are you,
Who grabbed my arm in a tight lock,
Before breaking it?

Which one are you,
Who defended the screams,
Cracking my back?

Which one are you,
Who had the courage to come,
Drag me from the room?

But you're not the hateful one.

Alastair J R Ball, Leicester, Leicestershire

PENSION DAY

I wait for my pension at the post office door,
Wishing and hoping it could be more.
Electric and gas and rent to pay.
Poll tax, the milkman, it all goes in one day.
It isn't much fun being old and hard up,
You tell younger people, they say "oh shut up"
The queues getting bigger, I look back and see,
All of these people are the same as me.
I say something funny, they all laugh and joke,
With a good sense of humour, I don't mind being broke.

Bridget Massey, Leicester, Leicestershire

MOTHER

One day in April
She planted forget-me-nots
She made me feel happy
Lots and lots.

She bought me sunshine
And I felt better
We made a little garden
Together.

I could hear her whisper
To every flower
The whole day passed by
Like an hour.

So I will press a forget-me-not
And send it with a pardon
For the years of misery I caused her
And remind her of our garden.

Kassia Green, Lutterworth, Leicestershire

MOTORWAY BLUES

Driving home,
weekend weary,
the slick surface hums
motorway blues.
Grey-steel thunderheads
squeeze the horizon
and nearing the city
a spatter of rain
patters the windscreen.

Suddenly, a golden halo
of light, damascene,
coronas the puff-edged clouds.
A split drips light
like spilt magnesium
from the towering masses,
and I drive
through a sharp, clear evening
towards the end of a rainbow.

Glenise Lee, Blaby, Leicestershire

SIMPLE

I lay in the thickness of night,
Playing ringlets upon her hair
And thinking
About how simple
It really is.

Mark Allen Gregory, Melton Mowbray. Leicestershire

SEA CREATURES

They swim about
In the ocean deep
Some are awake
Some are asleep.

Jellyfish, stingray
Still and silent
But if you be nasty
They'll turn violent.

Sharks on the other hand
Glide through the waters looking for their prey
Eating little fishes
All through the day.

There is one animal
I don't wish to be,
It's a fish
Because I don't want to be somebody's dinner dish.

Alina Main, Ibstock, Leicestershire

SCARED OF THE NIGHT

In my bed I lay
now it is night not day
the shadows in the corner
could be the shadow of the bogeyman
how silly it sounds
now the light chases away the imaginary groans
and the muffled moans
the chains clanking are just drains
the night sounds are just pains
with sleep comes nightmares
I wake up screaming but who cares?
not the knifeman
or the boys kicking cans
to them it's just a silly girlie having bad dreams
beneath the sleep roam monsters, bugs nasty and green
I never want to sleep
I don't want the light to go out
who knows what happens if you don't wake up in time
to hear the morning bells chime

Charlotte Thompson, Loughborough, Leicestershire

BESS

An ordinary little dog is she
Nothing remarkable there to see
But in fact she is bathed in a golden light
As one of God's messengers, sent for the plight
Of a small wayward girl who fell in distress
Into very deep water, soon followed by Bess
Who swam out to help in this time of great need
When your dog saves a life you feel humble indeed.

Dorothy Blakeman, Stamford, Lincolnshire

LONDON LAMENT

I won a trip to London, it's sometimes called "the smoke"
And while I travelled round the town I saw that was no joke.
The walls are black and grimy with no space in between.
It's interesting to visit, but I miss my Lincoln green.

I miss the sky so big and clear, the fields, the birds, the tractors.
I miss the friendly nods and waves and folk who've time to chat to us.
Down here they all look miserable and stare down at their feet.
They never look you in the eye when walking down the street.

If you say "good morning" they look at you quite queer.
Your cheery greeting's dangerous and fills them full of fear.
So I'm off back to Lincolnshire, the place that I call home.
To the fresh air, fields and friendly folk, I'll leave "the smoke" alone.

June Fitz Gibbon, Spilsby, Lincolnshire

SOMETIMES SOMETIMES

Sometimes you are good
Sometimes you are bad
Oh then you make me happy
Oh then you make me sad.

Sometimes you are so thoughtful
Sometimes you are so kind
Oh then you make me wish
Everything was yours and mine.

Sometimes you are awake all night
Sometimes you fall asleep
Sometimes you make me wonder
How much longer do you I have to keep.

Keith Powell, Skegness, Lincolnshire

Keith Leslie Powell said: "I was born in Darley Dale, Derbyshire in 1952. After attending Roe Farm Junior and Derwent Secondary Modern Schools until the age of 15, I worked upon my grandparents farm until it was sold in the late eighties. I then came to live in Skegness with my mother where I got into the poetry world by accident. As well as having a few poems published by many of the English poetry publishers, I have won the Lyric Prize at the 2000 Song Expo Benelux International Song and Culture Festival."

A TEAR

What is a tear? It is sadness and happiness rolled into one.
With emotions crossing over one another
As a tear falls so gently from one's eye that little drop of
water trickling down one's face
That drop of love to warm one's heart to show
that you care a tear of love is a bond that you can share
with others and others can share with you, a bringing
together an understanding a way of life.
To give hope for the future and to think love and life itself
is only a shadow in the dark a seed blowing in the wind.

Robin Morgan, Skegness, Lincolnshire

BLESSED DAWNING

I watch the sky that darkens
To midnight blue-and then
I see the moon that rises
With diamond stars all sparkling

Across the sky bright streaks of light
That shows that stars are falling.
Up to the north bright coloured shards
Of light are gaily dancing.
But then I see that golden orb
Of sun that is arising
Amid the wondrous clouds of white
A new day-it is dawning.

The birds that sing amongst the trees,
The cattle-they are lowing.
Young lambs are frolicking in the breeze
Young children-they are singing.

Maureen Fair, Heckington, Lincolnshire

FALLOUT

Early morning, pale light, frost-frozen
White lace webs spider-woven
Pale breath clouds the silent air.
Fingers of fog reach into rooms.
No bird-song, no paw-fall heard
Of cat or dog, nor tread of man.
Will the world end like this, frozen
Into utter stillness and calm?
After blast of bomb and rain of ash
The darkened earth will chill itself to death.

Margaret Todd, Burgh-le-Marsh, Lincolnshire

THE FARMHAND'S SON

He was born the son of a farmhand
Fated to follow the plough,
But he dreamed of leaving his own land
And gaining rare glory somehow.
So, thinking he'd grown into manhood.
He swore his life to the crown,
And forsaking his old life, his own blood.
Set off to defend distant towns.

Now nineteen years have fluttered by
On bleak, black corvid wings.
Denied are thoughts of those who've died,
For the grief and loss always stings.
But there's one memory that he won't let fade,
For he's an older and wiser man now.
And as he digs the graves of his comrades
He dreams of guiding the plough.

Paul Hughes, Grimsby, Lincolnshire

THE ARABIAN HORSE

The Arab is known for his endurance
Brilliant action and high performance
Noble swift and built for speed
Descendants from the desert seed
Streaming manes and tails held high
Gleaming silver in the sky
Surpassed all others he is fast
Faultless action to the last
Muscles tense with power and zeal
With tendon bones hard as steel
Stepping high with floating gait
Striding free he cannot wait
His hooves they barely touch the ground
A truly regal presence found
Dilated nostrils breathing fire
Brave courageous to admire
Truly grand entrancing sight
The Arabian herd with all its might
Galloped over desert sands
To disappear in foreign lands.

Catherine Armstrong, Skegness, Lincolnshire

Dedicated to the horse that made it all possible - Saul, nicknamed Shaziman.

Born in Manchester **Catherine Armstrong** enjoys playing the keyboard and accordion, gardening, riding and writing poetry. "I started writing poetry in 1972 after achieving a gold medal on my Arabian horse Saul in a long distance ride," she explained. "My work is influenced by my Christian faith and my style comes from the heart, portraying my life and my innermost thoughts." Aged 58 she has an ambition to be known through her poetry. Catherine has one daughter and the person she would like to be for a day is the Queen. "I would love to meet Ken Dodd because he makes me laugh so much," she said. "Happiness is so important in our lives."

REMEMBERING

In years to come, when you reminisce
When you think of me, while you gaze upon this,
When your heart starts to flutter,
And your mind has to roam
Don't ponder how life could have been,
As you sit by the fire alone,
It might not be any better,
It might even have ended up worse
Just enjoy the solitude's splendour
Whilst reading again each verse.

Robert Hunter, Grimsby, Lincolnshire

KINDRED EMOTIONS

Why does she feel love? how can this be?
Such beauty and perfection, falling for me?
I don't understand, I just cannot see,
Why would someone so perfect love me?

We met unexpectedly, out of the blue,
Maybe this fate thing is really true,
We opened right up, as if we were great friends,
After moments together we never wanted an end,

We're from such different places, and walks of life
But for the same things, we hope and we strive,
We have so much in common, kindred emotions
What good fortune to meet, so far over oceans,

I feel my life is better each day,
Thanks to a girl I met, so far away,
But to both live back here, it surely is fate,
Until I see her again, anxiously I wait.

Mitch Cokien, Grimsby, Lincolnshire

SIDELINE

Words came to me late one night,
Woke to write them with a light.
Poems come strange times of day,
Out of nowhere in my way.

I'll scald a tea-bag while I write
In the middle of the night
Then I'll climb back in my bed,
Hoping I can lose my head.

Into sleep, unthoughtful slumbers
Maybe dream of lucky numbers
Oh my luck I've overslept
Thank the silly words I've kept.

Ellen Eley, Horncastle, Lincolnshire

RIVER'S RUN

Feelings of foaming fury fill my mind
As your shimmering course falls freely past,
Searching nature's weakest way, so to find
Untrammelled progress, whether slow or fast,
Through gorges grim and dark deep mossy glades,
Unkissed by midday's sun's strong streaming rays.
And roaring on, not slowed as daylight fades,
Tumbling torrents, fresh-filled on rainy days
Fight furiously in tumultuous sound,
Your watery way fast-flowing, diving,
Spewing, slippery slide over boulders round,
Powerfully pounding, downward driving
Headlong in hot pursuit of open sea,
Fulfiling fretful, hard-earned destiny.

Paddy O'Neill, Woodhall Spa, Lincolnshire

WORSHIP

Do not worship a graven image
He said
It is not alive or dead
Just inanimate
Like a useless lump of lead
Throw it away instead

Do not worship the person in charge
It is only a woman or man
You are one too
And you
Could order them just as well
So do

But worship the woman you found
All the time
Time is not unending for you
Do not waste her life
Love your wife
This is true.

Donald Turner, Sleaford, Lincolnshire

Donald Turner said: "Living in Nottingham, city and county, for 62 years, I wrote poetry and prose occasionally. The only items published were in a railway staff magazine. Since moving to Lincolnshire, after retirement, I have written in a more systematic way, especially since founding and leading Sleaford U3A writing group. My usual subjects include humour, social comment, love, ageing problems and death, in other words, aspects of life. Some items have been published here and there, and one religious poem was commissioned and used at services. I live happily with my wife, Pamela, my pen at the ready."

TIDE

Rumbling pebbles
Sharp shifting sands
Ambient pounding of waves on the land
A small tumbling starfish
Skeletal hand
Vanishes in foam as the sea takes command
An intake of breath
The sea pulling back
A thunderous roar as the next wave attacks
Wind-blown spray dancing returns to the sea
To become once again
Vast energy.

Michael Doughty, Sleaford, Lincolnshire

AT THE END OF THE RAINBOW

Love at first sight, how I loved the girl.
Starting from the first time we dated.
On the dance floor, dancing with a whirl,
Rarely a wrong step, so elated.

Time passed slowly, then we were married.
We loved on honeymoon, so tender.
Later on a baby she carried.
How she blossomed in pregnant splendour.

When the time came she produced a boy.
Proudly she held him, for me to hold.
I was so happy, so full of joy
Worked all hours sent for my pot of gold.

Retirement came, a different life
With rainbows and at the end my wife.

Les Wiseman, Sleaford, Lincolnshire

ENCOUNTER

Rambling by the village of Lea
I was lost, as lost could be.
Then walking down a country lane.
I spied a man with a walking cane.
He appeared to be a local type
In farming clothes and old clay pipe.
I thought that he would know the way,
So I asked his advice, this very day,
"Why come o'er to bother me,
When there's a milestone by yon tree?"
I told him plainly as we spoke,
I cannot read and that's no joke.
He shook his head in great dismay,
"Y' canner read" I heard him say
"Then it's just for you, that milestone yon,
For it's one o' them sort, wi' nowt written on."

John Silkstone, Gainsborough, Lincolnshire

John Silkstone said: "I was born in Bolton, Lancashire in 1939 and now live in Lincolnshire. In 1956 I enlisted in the Army and in 1965 I married Jan and we had three wonderful daughters. I retired from the Army in 1981 and settled in Gainsborough. In April 2000 I enrolled on a Creative Writing course. My publications total four short stories, three articles and 46 poems. A collection of my stories and poems 'A Little Light Reading' (£3.50 includes p&p) is available from: J A Silkstone, Norwood House, 2 Bowling Green Road, Gainsborough, Lincolnshire, DN21 2QA."

FRAGMENT OF LOVE

Love is a fragment in our lives
Reaching out to us from the darkness
Spilling light from our hearts.
As the sun through a stained glass window.
The colours vibrant in its glow
There are only two that know
Two hearts, reaching out to wrap a rainbow of love
To hold on to the joy, the happiness for a while.
The ecstasy, the pain, the hurt, there's no denial.
Love is a fragment in our lives.

Blanche Middleton, Skegness, Lincolnshire

STARRY NIGHTS

What magic works on moonless nights?
In sequinned cluttered skies
Such majesty within our sights
What wonder greets our eyes?

A velveteen valance that abounds
With hues of gun-metalled blue
Suspent from heaven our earth surrounds
Enhancing the glittering view

Whose worlds are these that meet our gaze
That pulse through inconceivable time
What like their night what like their days
Be they any different than mine?

Do they look out from there to here?
In the self-same ignorance
As we look out from here to there
A spellbound audience.

Peter Jennings, Grimsby, Lincolnshire

HARPER

I heard a harper just the other day,
Oh how I wished that I could play,
He stepped his tunes, oh how he sang
Above the bells for mass that rang.

I watched the ragged millionaire
That danced and played without a care,
And all the world was bright and gay
Just the once, just that day.

I heard a girl singing her pleasure
As he subtled out his measure
And me just left in state of trance
Feet that could naught else, but dance.

Over the hills and far and gone
But my feet they will go dancing on,
And that colleen still she's singing
With shadows of his notes, still ringing.

A child in its mother's shawl
Has ceased to wail he claps, and all
That's beaming on his tiny face
Imaginary harp, his fingers trace.

John Sullivan, Grimsby, Lincolnshire

LIFE*

All my life my heart has beat
Silence would be deadly
For the thumping pulse to cease

Every hour on the chime
Clock ticking every second
The world would stop, if it were to lose its voice

For eternity the world has turned
But if I could stop the spinning
Would it pause?
Or would it end?
Or would I be reborn?

Joanne Brandon, Glentham, Lincolnshire

ALIVE

When your eyes start getting dimmer
And your life begins to simmer
Instead of boil
You're not getting any slimmer
And you rather think a zimmer
Is getting near
Your back complains each time you bend
All you can do is try and mend
With massage oil
You get a pain and heaven forfend
Is this the beginning of the end?
Never fear
Thanks to the Lord above
And all those near that you love
You're alive.

Patricia Pickworth, Louth, Lincolnshire

THREE HAIKU

Windswept autumn sighs
Scattering bronze confetti
For winter's bridal.

Cats sneak like shadows,
Obsequious assassins
In silken disguises.

Thoughts tumble and spin
In brain's deft machinery,
Then hang out to dry.

Moonyeen Blakey, Cleethorpes, Lincolnshire

THE END

They hurt you, then move on
These creatures of this land
They have no cares no worries.
You are putty in their hands
They enjoy every minute every plan.
Every twist and every turn.
Their power is such, you would never learn
Keeping you weak is what makes them so strong
They're always right and you're always wrong
You bear the cruel things they say and do.
And when you are beat you feel guilty for being so weak
Stay away, no more pain and you get to sleep again.
Defeated you've given in.
Now watch the lemmings gather.
Around the workplace bully
For they always win.

Sally Chappell, Spalding, Lincolnshire

CAN SPRING BE FAR BEHIND?

We soon will hear the sounds of spring
When happy folk come out to sing
That bleak cold winter now is routed,
Despite the showers
It's never doubted.

Old nature plays her yearly jest
With cuckoo egg in warbler's nest
And birds swoop down to snatch at crumbs
And pounce with glee,
On unwary worms.

And churchly hands will polish brass
Trim the hedges and tend the grass
Out of the belfry flies the bat
Away from the cleaning,
And all of that.

New blossoms find themselves unfurled
Into a flower-hungry world
And small seeds stir beneath the earth
Preparing themselves
For life's rebirth.

Jeannie Peck, Louth, Lincolnshire

LE PETIT SENSATION

Deep in a vague dark pool
Small star dimly shines
Waiting for deeper night
To shimmer spread constellations
Where it will be queen

Time is strange; I look up
The quiet sky is full of dawn

                Michael Fry, Caythorpe, Grantham, Lincolnshire

FRIENDS

Friends are important to you and me,
For all this is plain to see
We love to sit and share,
And to listen and hear.
All our friends love us too,
As we love them through and through.

Friends are necessary in life
To help us through battles and strife.
The love you give them, they can store,
And give it back when the battles you endure.
Our friends are special in our life,
We are there for each other in our strife.

Your friends journey along the road with you,
Whether it is many miles or just a few.
To your friends nothing matters at all,
You are there for each other's beck or call.
Without our friends our life would be so dull,
So it is good to have many, to make our life full.

                Mary Clark, Immingham, Lincolnshire

HOUSE RULES

Why is it there must be rules
like don't put mud on your shoes
Don't put paint on your skirt
leaving fingerprints on your shirt?

Red sauce, flying down the dress
and leaving the house in a horrible mess.

Paper cups stacked up under the bed
and not be forgetting to feed Fred.

Little things like letters flying out the window
to police, sticking out a finger
writing this all down isn't a joke
as I have told this to nearly choke.

Baking tins must dry properly else they will rust
don't touch, electrical plugs else your
father gives you a thick ear.

Don't leave down your hair
else wasp and bees will hang in there.

Why so many rules,
when I want to play and choose?

Amanda Renyard, Townside, Lincolnshire

A KIND OF MAN

When all the waves of grief have calmed,
And as our tears subside,
We'll see the man who still remains,
He's gone but hasn't died.

He is in his children's faces,
In his grandchildren's eyes,
The kind of man who's here and now
Not one who leaves and dies.

He's in the music that we hear,
A great part of his life,
In daily cherished memories of,
His ever-loving wife.

He's in the funny anecdotes,
Told endlessly by friends,
He is in the summer sunshine,
In autumn's coloured blends.

He is in the winter beauty,
In spring's fresh, brand-new days,
He's not the kind of man who dies,
But one who lives always.

Hayley Nixon, Friskney, Lincolnshire

Born in Derbyshire **Hayley Nixon** enjoys writing and reading poetry as well as listening to music. "I started writing poetry in my early teens," she remarked. "It was a way of getting ideas and feelings out of my system without having to talk about them. I would like to be remembered as a thought-provoking poet and a devoted wife and mother." Aged 31, Hayley is married to Kevin and they have four children. "The person I would most like to be meet is Maya Angelou so that I could tell her how wonderful her poems are and how she inspires the masses," said Hayley. "As well as short stories and songs I have written many poems and had several published."

WHO ELSE WILL IT BE?

If it's not to be me
Then who else will it be?
I, who thought myself lucky
To be thrown a few crumbs of kindness
Which soon blew away
Like cobwebs in corners
Not meant to be there
Guiltily blown to shreds
After the spider's hard play.

So who will it be
Now it's not me?
I stare in the mirror.
As I'm slowly replaced
There smiles my old spirit
With eyes open wide
The spectre of victim displaced.
The cool breeze of new beginnings
Lifts me
Taking me along
Like a magic carpet
To a new place.....
Freedom.

Carol Ann Baker, Grimsby, Lincolnshire

Dedicated to mum, dad and Andy, Michelle, Mark and Sophie. I love you. x

Born in Grimsby, **Carol Ann Baker** enjoys writing and DIY. "I started writing poetry at the age of ten, inspired by my English teacher," she explained. "My poetry is influenced by this teacher and also major events in my life and my style is simple and uncomplicated, coming from the heart. I would like to be remembered as someone who was easy to get along with and treated people as I would wish to be treated." Aged 43, Carol is a child minder, with an ambition to earn a living as a newspaper columnist. She has three children and the people she would most like to meet are the songwriting team of Elton John and Bernie Taupin. "My biggest fantasy is to have enough money to buy a villa in Spain and spend half of the year there!" she said.

OH TO BE A SAINT

Oh, how I'd like to be a saint
Something I certainly ain't
To be an angel will do fine
If I could be nice all the time
I try hard to be kind and good
Something I know I should
Things just don't work out my way
Watching what I do and say
Someone deliberately causes me hurt
Then rubs my face in the dirt
They stick in the knife a few times more
Now it's time to declare war
Only when all's said and done
I realise they've really won
'Cos I've lowered myself to their level
Fair sprouted horns, like a devil
Shouldn't let my tongue run away
Saying those thing I ought not say
So bang goes my halo and wings
Guess I never was meant for such things.

Margaret Debnam, Grimsby, Lincolnshire

RED

No bright red flickering fire on a cold winter's night,
Or shepherd's delight illuminating the cloudy sky.
No brightly-bricked houses standing proud on the street,
No lit up nose and cheeks in the cold,
No sore red eyes, or a robin's red breast.
Only one colour of apple on the market stall.
No shiny red hearts, or roses bright,
What would the world be like without red?

Martin Samson, Grantham, Lincolnshire

MONEY

Money is a dangerous thing, the root to all greed,
Placed in a building society, it's the planting of a seed.

People want loads of it, they just can't get enough
Bits of paper and metal can buy all kinds of stuff.

Most people work hard for it, they earn their fair keep,
Others climb in through windows and take it while you sleep.

Those that have lots of it buy big homes and cars,
Those that diddle it find themselves behind bars.

The value of it is changing every minute, every day
£4 per hour is what employers have to pay.

It has been around for many years, but will it ever go?
Pound, sterling or the euro, I somehow think no.

Paul Russell, Boston, Lincolnshire

VINCENT'S TREE

In my dawn I see your tree.
In the way that you used to
The colours are many for me to see.
Orange, purple, green, yellow or blue?
Changing, changing all about my early view.
It's between two buildings of wood and brick,
Chimney pots are mingled in.
The varied birds that I can see,
Are flying over and under,
And then towards me.

Janet Petchey, Grimsby, Lincolnshire

MY SISTER, MY SELF

In that fleeting moment in time,
The earth had ceased to rotate,
And I saw a face not unlike
My own.

Somewhere in another place,
Endlessly she seemed to wait,
I was her
And she was me.

Did we share the same emotions, then?
Did she know that moment,
Our souls touched
And that instant I knew...

She was my sister,
Or myself,
From a different past or future...
Though what or which I could not tell.

Sophie Nuttall, Holton-le-Clay, Lincolnshire

BEAR ESSENTIALS

Watching from a distance; eyes follow everywhere,
I don't feel uncomfortable even though he stares;
Never passes comment, wouldn't ever dream to judge,
Sits completely still and listens, doesn't even budge,
The only person in my life I can completely trust;
Confidante and soul mate his friendship is a must;
I class myself as single; I go out alone;
I know I can rely on him to be there when I get home;
Had too much to drink; undressing is a task;
Where I have been he won't presume to ask;
Waiting in bed to cuddle when I'm ready;
Unconditional love that only comes from teddy.

Linda Thurling, Louth, Lincolnshire

A PRICELESS FROLIC

Lick my lilac flower,
Golden boy.
Concentrate your raining gaze
On the underside of petal,
Golden boy,
Wink not, stop not your long stare,
Point your hair,
Golden boy;
And the purple head appears
To link golden our match.
My growth dependent on your scorching touch,
I wear
My stems in paler green,
Petals adorned with golden gear,
And yearn for more of
Your relieving fare,
Golden boy.

Yuriy Humber, Grimsby, Lincolnshire

PARTYING

She made a commotion as I tabled her motion
and put a big smile on her face
She's in the political arena and you've probably seen her
She's at rallies all over the place
I've read her agenda and know how to bend her
So she follows my party line
And I can make her strip without a three-line whip
Her portfolio looks just fine
She's honed to perfection for the next by-election
Then she'll give a surgery
And on her surgery table she'll show me she's able
to be more than just an MP.

Jim White, Grimbsy, Lincolnshire

TATTOOS

He has love tattooed on four fingers
And hate on four
The world's two most important words
Displayed on eight digits.

And I wonder which came first?
And why he must display his life
So openly, so publicly
Buying a lottery ticket
Or boarding a bus.

And is the love
Part of the broken heart
Tattooed above his left elbow?

Or the minute one
Hiding beneath his right cuff
Which says simply mum.

Patricia Crouter, Cleethorpes, Lincolnshire

BEAUTY

I lie in a place far, far away,
But beauty still is around me.
Looking in the sky so blue,
While birds fly around me.

Clouds go by in colours so gay,
But beauty still surrounds me.
Moving fast, moving slow,
Changing position and shapes.
That's why beauty surrounds me.

Like in a race fast and slow,
I wish I could move like the clouds so blue.
Leaving my troubles behind me.

Kenneth Chapman, Grimsby, Lincolnshire

Kenneth Freeman Raymond Chapman said "I have been writing poetry for as long as I can remember. My early influences came from my career as a professional footballer when I played with and against some of the best England had to offer. Today I am inspired by Tennyson and visiting places of outstanding natural beauty. I am a compulsive writer and often have to stop what I am doing to write down what comes in my mind. I have a large collection of poetry and also children's stories."

A WARNING TO YOU, MY FRIEND

Beware my friend,
Of the dangers in the wood,
The list doesn't have an end,
Read them, you really should.

For what lives there,
Are many dangerous creatures,
Such as the terrifying luminous bear,
Who has many terrifying features.

You may have heard
Of the bloodsucking bat,
Who simply looks absurd,
Well he lives there, fancy that.

So, beware my friend,
Of the dangers in the wood,
Otherwise you could come to an end,
Read the list of dangers, you really should.

Cath Nelms, Sleaford, Lincolnshire

Cath Nelms said: "I'm 13 and really want to be a famous writer when I'm older. My English teacher says I'm good at writing poems and stories, and I hope everyone else says the same too. I enjoy reading, and after I read 'Alice in Wonderland' and 'Alice Through the Looking Glass', I found the inspiration to write this poem. If I could meet Lewis Carol I would want to say a big thank you."

COMMAS AND COLONS

Oh what prisons are in punctuation,
Ever-shackling zealous screeds.
Undo me from this consummation.

Asterisks blank in constellation,
Alight me where the comma seeds.
Oh what prisons are in punctuation.

Speech marks deaf to education,
Quote exclamation's sullen breeds.
Undo me from this consummation.

The sentence parsed in mitigation;
Insidious verb that slyly speeds.
Oh what prisons are in punctuation.

One by one the Grammar Nation,
Elect against the poet's deeds.
Undo me from this consummation.

Blindfolded Muse in suffocation,
Prepares her ruin in rebel weeds.
Oh what prisons are in punctuation.
Undo me from this consummation.

Francis McDermott, Cleethorpes, Lincolnshire

Dedicated to Jessie Walker of Blackness Court, Dundee. Thank you.

THE FLY

The fly is a two winged insect, its colour mostly black,
It has enormous energy, it's never, never slack.
Whether it is nervous, hungry or just bored, I am unable to assess,
But its frenetic busyness, is an irritation quite intense.

The fly is really quite a pretty thing, it's exquisitely sheen,
But it has disgusting habits, so repulsive and obscene,
It searches far and wide to find excreta, or horse droppings of manure,
Then flits around your house, to taste your meat, bread or sugar.

Not only is it never still, but disgorges what's ingested.
It's natures way to keep it slim, or so it's been suggested,
It doesn't need a laxative, it defecates by day and night,
A most attractive visitor. Why would we wish to swat it?

The spider works hard to spin a web, to arrest it in its fling,
Does it have sadistic tendencies, and like to see it swing?
We shall never know what motivates the spider to his prey,
But one less flitting round the house, it's hip, hip, hooray.

Elizabeth Chivers, Grimsby, Lincolnshire

Born in London **Elizabeth Chivers** enjoys playing bridge, gardening, embroidery and writing sketches and poems. "I only started writing three years ago when I joined a writers' group," she pointed out. "This gave me the inspiration to create and my work is influenced by everyday things. I write about them just as I see them. I would describe my style as humorous and thought-provoking." Elizabeth is a retired nurse and as well as sketches for concerts she has written several poems.

THE DOLPHIN

O joyous creature of the deep, how you thrill me when you leap,
From ocean's depth to high in air. You seem to neither know nor care,
Of this world's problems and its pain, for ever since the days of Cain,
Men have killed through hate and greed, and none, it seems, can quite succeed,
In living peaceably like you, loving, trusting, caring too.
O dolphin, tell me if you can, is there any hope for man?
Will we one day be blithe and free, rejoicing in our liberty?
Free spirit of the oceans wide, you have no need to turn and hide,
For you are perfect of your kind; joyful, faithful, pure of mind.
It's you whom we should emulate. You, who never learned to hate,
But greet all comers with a smile, and choose to linger a while;
And when the good Lord fashioned you, I'm sure that He was smiling too.

Joan Daines, Freiston, Boston, Lincolnshire

HOW THE FAITHFUL FALL

Temptation is an ancient evil
Empty minds an easy target
Marriages of truth are lost when
Promises hold deep excitement
Trust grows thin and breeds aggression
Ammunition verbally thrown
Tears cascade and drown allegiance
Invisible tempter knows he's won
Obituary lists love and loyalty
Neither the greater of curiosity

     Sarah Clift, Grimsby, Lincolnshire

REMEMBERING

My childhood days
Happy laughing
Through each day.

Time rolls on, growing up
Work for me has now begun
A daily happy song.

Time has passed me by again
Now it's days of rest.
As I look out of the window
See the children playing in the sand.

I turn away remembering
Resting in my chair.

That was my childhood days.

     E M Wright, Spalding, Lincolnshire

Dedicated to my granddaughter, Helen Wright, for her kindness, love and caring ways.

THE BEST GIFTS

As I opened my presents it occurred to me,
That the best gifts of all we don't always see,
Like the kindly word when you're feeling low,
Or that friendly smile that warms you so.
The sweet concern that soothes your pain,
Hands that help you back to your feet again.
So throughout the year let us try to be
A little more thoughtful to those we see.
To take a little time to share
Those heavy burdens so hard to bear.
All these are precious gifts of love
That will help us serve our Father above.
They may not be wrapped in paper gay
But can lift your heart and lighten your way.

Lyndis Smith, Boston, Lincolnshire

Born in Fleetwood **Lyndis Smith** enjoys writing and embroidery. "I started writing poetry only recently," she explained. "Some friends started a small writers' group and this inspired me to pick up my pen. My work is influenced by my feelings and my faith and my style is contemplative. I would like to be remembered as a good, supportive friend who was always ready to help." Aged 64, Lyndis is retired and is married to Charles. They have two sons, Christopher and Nicholas. "As well as short stories I have written many poems and made up my own book," she added.

IN HINDSIGHT

Never really got into religion and stuff
First they asked me to pray
At least twice every day
Then they read the Commandments which I must obey
And that was enough

Had no faith in pretentious political stuff
Like the vows to redress
The distressed NHS
And they promised less tax, a full one per cent less
Which wasn't enough

Didn't trust anyone. As for marriage and stuff
How could that ever be
An advantage to me
When I'd always been happy to cook my own tea?
Well, happy enough

Only ever believed in myself. You can stuff
All your spiritual healing
And your false fellow-feeling
Compared with your life, mine was far more appealing
But... was it enough?

Caroline Burton, Grimsby, Lincolnshire

GLITTERED SKIES

Sing to me,
sweet siren sky.
Rest those weary eyes
of mine
and carry me,
beneath your wing,
as the night goes by.

And if I shall wake
before the sun has risen.
And all I see is night,
may the stars soothe me
back to sleep
beneath the glittered skies.

James McCarron, Alford, Lincolnshire

SILENT STRANGER

I lie here with you by my side
You want to speak and yet cannot
I understand. Taking your hand; comfort.
Our hands and hearts are not strangers
But our two bodies although next to each other
Have never been so far apart. Partnership.
Although you smile them away into your nightmares,
I can read the tears in your eyes.
You worry the words will push me away.
The force of truth, grown with strength through
Its many years, practising the moment.
I don't love you conditionally, the past still
Haunts many a mortal creature.
I will love you, even when you can speak the words
You dare not let slip into consciousness.
For I too have read them in your eyes.

Kathryn Ditcher, Bourne, Lincolnshire

BLOODY KIDS

They come screaming into our world, bloody kids.
Like bundles of fury that knock on the door,
From nappies to knicks that contain smelly skids.
Won't someone please tell me, why do we have more?

Linda Stapleton, Boston, Lincolnshire

ALADDIN'S CAVE

If the ground had been soft when Humpty fell,
There would have been no nursery rhyme to tell.
If Jack's bean had matured not,
The giant would have been no more than a blot.
If Wee Willie Winkie had retired when he ought,
In the town in his nightgown he wouldn't be caught.
If in the web the spider had lingered and stayed,
Miss Muffet's fright might have been delayed.
If to kiss the girls Georgie hadn't tried,
He wouldn't have run, and they wouldn't have cried.
If Grandma to judo or karate had gone,
Red Riding Hood's story might have been a different one.
If Cinderella had been more bold and hearty,
She'd have locked up the sisters and spoiled their party.
If the cat had played the flute instead of the fiddle,
The cow jumping over the moon wouldn't have been such a riddle.
So if all the rhymes were differently told,
In Aladdin's cave, it would have been mud not gold.

Shirley Lowater, Butterwick, Boston, Lincolnshire

LOVERS' LANE

They call it lovers' lane.
Tall trees, so green.
Oh so, just the same
As it was years ago.
As we wander through by the little stream,
Still rippling, murmuring on its way
Sunshine shone down.
As you hold my hand
In the same old way.
Time has passed
But our love had lasted
From day after day.
And we strolled on down lovers' lane.

Beryl Manning, Cleethorpes, Lincolnshire

Born in Cleethorpes **Beryl Manning** enjoys reading, writing and walking. "I started writing poetry in my teens because I found I enjoyed doing it," she said. "I would describe my style as sentimental and sad and I would like to be remembered as a loving and caring person." Aged 68, Beryl is a housewife. She is married to David and they have one daughter and two grandchildren. "I have written some short stories and had several poems published," she said. "The people I would most like to meet are the Queen and Elvis Presley. My biggest fantasy is having my own castle to live in with my family. My worst nightmare is having another heart attack."

MORTIFIED

This choking is back,
It's tearing me up,
There's nothing I want,
But feelings of luck.

Why won't it leave?
Will it never decease,
I'm getting this feeling,
Almost every eve.

More and more often,
Is this feeling around,
I wish it would go,
Back down in the ground.

Why does this happen?
What is the source?
Never again,
Will I follow this force.

Johnathan Keating, Middle Rasen, Lincolnshire

A VIEW

The timeless yet old Victorian house
With its massive front porch
And brown shady dog
With lamplight shining brightly
Across the road
The sprightly girl practices her ice dance routine
As if by nature set
On the pure glass pond
The man from the Victorian house blows his flute louder
The girl beckons him across as she possesses the ice
To dance to the clear and pleasant flute music

Jennifer Dunkley, Grimsby, Lincolnshire

ENOUGH

Some ask for the moon and the stars
Whenever the going gets tough.
Others crave boundless riches
When all that they need is,
Enough.

When loved ones enquire,
How strong is your love?
Don't give them a swift rebuff.
Just take them gently in your arms
And tell them,
Enough.

For that's all we require,
Tho' life can sometimes get rough.
We ask ourselves.
How much are our needs?
The answer,
Enough is enough.

Ernest Barrett, Wainfleet, Lincolnshire

THE HANGING TREE

White-bleached branches, leafless hulk
cold caressing creak, wooded bulk
breathing beneath storm-cast sky
fear's companion, staring socket eye
blackened bark, bare-stripped bone
raucous raven guardian stands alone
drawing tight black-feathered cloak
burdened bough, death's whispered croak
echoing ghosts, spirits' silent screams
invading image fills unwelcome dreams
straining sinew, swinging hanging rope
shrivelled skin, breaking strangled hope
gnarled, twisted trunk, lightning scarred
pecked flesh fragment, scattered shard
dangling corpse, blood dried black
sun-shrunken hide, tightened slack
twirling below rain's drizzled stench
drifted draught, foul rotting stench
restless rustling, sound gently borne
brushing cobwebbed threads, nightmare's dawn

Paul Birkitt, Blyton, Gainsborough, Lincolnshire

IF LOVE WERE A FLOWER

If love were a flower
what should it be?
an elegant rose
or the cheerful daisy?
a violet perhaps
the word love it contains
the sweet-scented lily, no, its pollen stains
or even an iris
perhaps the carnation
which always appears whatever the occasion
if love were a flower
what should it be?
a flower in heaven growing for eternity

H Charlton, Boston, Lincolnshire

LOVE

Think of me not far away
In quiet moments of the day
Whispers in the rustling leaves
Touching cheeks on the breeze
High among the stars each night
Feel my love burning bright
I am with you every day
Think of me not far away

Howard Marshall, Grimsby, Lincolnshire

Howard Marshall said: "I am an artist first, painting mainly abstracts. Only in the last two years have I started to write verse. This is the first poem I have had printed. I would like to publish my own collection of poems eventually, but writing seems to take second place to painting."

LIGHT OF MY LIFE

He's the light of my life, I'm not scared to say
My love for him grows stronger each day
We only got together to have a good time
I never thought that he would be mine

He changed my life and turned it around
His love for me knows no bounds
He cared and it showed and this was new
So my love for him just grew and grew

He is always there my strength and my rock
He picks me up when life gives a knock
He is quiet, kind and incredibly calm
His aim is to protect me so I come to no harm

He would lay down his life, of this I am sure
How could I ask for anything more?
He is my world I want to shout
He is all that I need or care about

Gill Doyle, Bracebridge Heath, Lincolnshire

CLIFF WALL

Weather-beaten and submissive
To the fickle force of the elements
Here is the end border of country,
The calloused face of tidal barricades.

Standing high above water,
A dolmen of immense size
Casting its natural magic
Across the darkening expanse of sea.

It fails to meet its own reflection
In the green translucence of the tides.
Its eyes, blind by ages
Spent watching nothing but the waves
Hide a contempt for the ocean.

But despite such lofty defiance
The beating spray enacts a terrible price,
As each encroaching passage of elements
Serves to remove, piece by piece
The cliff wall's being.

Daniel Stannard, Kettering, Northamptonshire

A SEED OF DOUBT ONCE PLANTED

A seed of doubt once planted,
Will surely take root one day,
Until it has consumed or destroyed,
And pushed our love away.

And somewhere on the beautiful blue,
I sail and do my job,
While my heart is miles and miles away,
Filled with heartaches and tearful sobs.

I utter a prayer once told me,
Of history and its course,
Yet little help from above,
Has removed my feeling of remorse.

In a place where one can do nothing,
Only accept things as they come,
The mind becomes acute with thought,
And at the same time becomes numb.

Pia Edwards, Northampton, Northamptonshire

Thank you Richard for coming into my life and bringing calmness and tranquillity. You make me happy and alive.

Pia Edwards said: "I have been writing verse for eight years and I am strongly influenced by love of travel. I am currently working as a Police Officer so often need time to escape. I go off and explore where I can, to relax and write. My father inspired me to write when I was a young child, as he writes himself. I started writing more when I lived in America so that I could reminisce about home. I hope to spend some time in Asia and one day become a great detective."

NO SALE

Red pouting lips
Blue shadowed eyes.
Sidelong glances
Upthrusting thighs

Flesh boldly showing
Almost to the church
And that with decoration
Inviting one to touch

All this to try arousing
Sex, without a soul
Sadly advertising
Just an empty hole.

John Howlett, Daventry, Northamptonshire

SEPTEMBER 11TH

A dark cloud prevails over some of our world
Not a word is spoken or a sound can be heard
As we all sit in silence in respect of the city
And we pray for lost souls
With our love and our pity

United we stand in grief and in pain
As we all know our lives will not be the same
So special is life a thing to be treasured
Each minute, each hour just cannot be measured

And now as we mourn the ones who have gone
Let them live in our hearts
And let their memory live on.

Wendy Holliday, Kingsthorpe, Northamptonshire

THE VALUE OF TIME

Time, the master of us all,
we must answer to his call.
The fifth, the binding element,
the one that we are only lent.
He is the single lasting power,
the one who all before must cower.
Not fire, not water, nor earth or air,
no one exists that may stand and dare.
Not life, not death, or gods on high.
Time, immortal, only is,
take this time, you've borrowed his.

Amanda Louise Fisher, Northampton, Northamptonshire

MOMENT

Gods of time slow
This moment for me
Make it drag like
A tired working day

My prayer will fall on
Autumn leaves
Silent as a long-forgotten
Song
In a morning breeze

I have no time for this moment
It's gone before
I can catch
A delicate breath
In the sad land
Where this moment
Cannot be.

Simon Arch, Kettering, Northamptonshire

IN THE STONE-FACED CITY STREETS

Stony frozen pathways,
The egotistical malice of our profane age.
Picture the withered flower of humility,
Crushed amidst their imperial marbled stone.

The illusion of possessions serves,
Their neurotic faithless void of a heart
Believers in a materialism, infallible.
Generating multiples of crystal palaces.

The masonry limestone cut from time,
Bones of the poor and weak crushed to dust.
All to build prisons of Samsâra.
Their monument to the slavery of the masses.

William Milligan, Corby, Northamptonshire

Born in Kettering **William Milligan** has interests including playing the harmonica, motorcycling and painting. "I started writing poetry when I was 14," he remarked. "Reading George Orwell made me politically aware about the world and my work is influenced by the beat poets of the fifties as well as nature. I would like to be remembered as a poet who connected his mind to all categories of people and was always genuine to the written word." Aged 32, William is a shift worker with ambitions to become a successful poet and to write a novel. "I am working on a book and have written many poems," he said. "The person I would most like to meet is the writer Michael Moorcock because I am fascinated by his unique writing style."

THE MAGIC BOX

I will put in the box
The last tooth from a Xuanhanosaurus,
A sparkling moon reflecting in the ocean,
And the first autumn leaf that appears.
I will put in the box
The rolling waves of the world,
The first shooting star in the atmosphere,
And the wings of a butterfly

Victoria Ryder, Rushden, Northamptonshire

A SPECTRUM OF EMOTIONS

Inside a person,
A shower of emotions
All reds and blues and greens,

Red is all angry,
But spotted with love
It cries and simmers and dreams,

Blue is deep losses,
The races not won,
It hides until called to use,

Green is all envy
With hatred a-swirl,
Green is just used to abuse,

There are colours inside,
These the most common,
All reds and blues and greens.

Laura Sutcliffe, Brackley, Northamptonshire

SMALL POEM IN OCTOBER

Of my love I would sing if I could
Flight of golden birds
I would paint my love
Jewel colours gold an altarpiece.

Enfold me and I will weep my love
Weep weep weep my love
For the sheer strength of it
But I can dance dance my love.

Denise Sampson, Northampton, Northamptonshire

DAYBREAK

Swirling early mist
Shrouds village church steeple,
Bells ring their message.

Red streaking the sky,
World turning, dawn breaking
Birds chorus greeting.

Dawn's golden sunlight
On white frosted landscape
Shines on winter scene.

Bright golden sunrays.
Winter's illumination
Of white frosted fields.

Huge orange-red sphere
Rises over horizon
Morning has broken.

Joyce Buksh, Kettering, Northamptonshire

MUM

Although you are not here today
My memories of you will always stay
Within my heart, within my mind
To me dear mum you were so kind.

Your love was real and close to my heart
That's why it was hard for us to part
Of all mothers you were the best
But now God has taken you home to rest.

Yvonne Bodily, Northampton, Northamptonshire

My mum was my closest friend and guide. This poem is dedicated to her memory. She was my inspiration.

SO CLOSE

To find the peace,
To free my mind,
And end the struggle
On this final page, unfinished,
I am so... close.

To purge the guilt,
To break the bonds,
And fly reborn
From all that went before,
I am so... close.

To walk in light,
To leave the past,
And shed the yoke
Of burdens, deep within,
I am so... close.

Janet Sheffield, Northampton, Northamptonshire

NIGHTFALL

How sharp the edge of night
How cold its unwelcome edge prevails
It falls like an Noachian deluge
Some cower before its inky mantle
While others bathe in its melano
The wolf howls the owl hoots shadows arise
The goat-sucker emerges as the bat shrill
Echoes through the night
The cockerel heralds the disedging of night
As night skulks away before the dawn
To sharpen another edge of night

Michael Lawler, Northampton, Northamptonshire

A WARM BED ON A COLD NIGHT

Electric blankets leave me cold
I'd rather have something I can hold
A full-length hot water bottle is what I need.
My husband won't volunteer.

I stand in the kitchen watching the kettle
Waiting for the water to boil.
There's something that makes me think of Mum
Making the hot water bottle.

Flannelette sheets feel warm and furry
Warm patch where the bottle's been.
Bedsocks keep both feet toasty
I snuggle under the eiderdown.

It's cold outside, frosty and clear
But I don't mind tonight.
Warm sheets, warm feet and something to cuddle
I've got my bottle, goodnight.

Kym Wheeler, Corby, Northamptonshire

DO YOU CARE?

Do you care
If a child screams next door,
Mummy don't please don't
A mother in despair
At the end of her tether
Knocking her child to the floor?

Do you care
When you see someone mugged.
Do you pass on the other side
Because you cannot abide
Interfering in others' affairs?

Do you care
When a child dies in Kampuchea,
Somalia or God knows where.
Impoverished by war and drought
Is that what it's all about?

Do you love the human face.
No matter what colour it is?
Or are you wrapped up
In your own little place,
A bundle of prejudice?

Elaine Perry, Yardley Gobion, Northamptonshire

SEPARATION

The phone rang and he was there
'Was I all right' and did I care?
I had driven all day but he was tired

He phoned again, why didn't I reply?
You were busy and so am I
Remember I drove all day and you were tired

I phoned him, the question the same
So was the answer, and for shame
Where is trust, is it lost in control?

Absence of trust seals the fate
Or did I merely swallow the bait
Did he or I put an end to this game?

Where control comes first and trust is lost
Lives at alien mercies, are heaved and tossed
And alas, poor love's seed cannot survive

So be it, it is at an end
As our separate ways we wend
And do I really care?

Stuart Griffey, Duston, Northamptonshire

BUTTERFLY

The wings of a butterfly,
So colourful, delicate.
I watch the sun reflecting,
Blues, yellows, brilliant whites.
Gliding, arching, swaying,
Caught on a summer breeze.
Twirling, swirling, curling,
What a dazzling sight.
So dainty, fragile,
The wings of a butterfly.

Michelle Rae, Corby, Northamptonshire

A VALENTINE

My love for you I can't confine
To this one day of Valentine
But I would like another way
To pass the message of this day

Can it be that I might find
A new way to say what's on my mind?
Is there another way to define
The message of St Valentine?

Try as I do with all my might
Lying awake through all the night
I cannot find another phrase
To explain why my heart's in such a daze.

Try as I might the truth is this
Nothing more and nothing less
Old words are best, there are no new
To tell the message - I LOVE YOU!

Duncan Johnstone, Northampton, Northamptonshire

THE WHITE HART

At the foot of terraced slope
the white hart starts;
his head held high in alarm
muscles braced for flight.

He leaps high over the mossy gate,
then as a marble statue gazes
from the edge of the dark forest
at the danger above.

Leafy greenness enfolds him,
leaving in that ancient dell
only sharp hoof prints
to speak of his presence.

Tall trees sigh in the wind
buzzards cry overhead.
All else is still
melting into Oneness of Being.

Anne Rutherford, Corby, Northamptonshire

NECTAR AT DAWN

At the unfurling of the dawn
As the dew begin to form
A silver veil to deliver
That will glisten and shimmer
As the morning begins to warm
And the fragrance is borne
To float with such a flair
On the stirrings of the air
To every flower leaf and blade
A caress will be made
A drop of nectar is born
In this iridescent dawn

Diane Kennedy, Northampton, Northamptonshire

KAREN

Till you came into my life it was empty and barren
An angel sent to earth, they christened you Karen
With eyes of blue and enchanting face
No finer example of the human race
Your personality is infectious, it stands out a mile
In your company I can't help but smile
Your voice is soothing calm and sweet
No one better, couldn't wish to meet
To describe how I'm feeling is impossible to do
Till something sounds better than
I love you

Robert Wright, Gt Cransley, Northamptonshire

Dedicated to Karen Elizabeth Hartley (K.E.H.).

EPPING FOREST IN MY POCKET-BOOK

Centuries of leaves
In a cathedral of trees
Carpeted with breeze

Alone in a crowd
Light dim, a face peers out
From a crumpled skin

Leaf fall glittering
Autumn sunlight flickering
Black crows bickering

Cascading deadfall
A jackpot of leaf pennies
A blanket of gold

A shower of sunlight
Tall canopy filtering
Sun-streaked whispering winds

Colin Slater, Polebrook, Northamptonshire

Colin Slater said: "I am a professional painter of atmospheric landscapes which express the experience of walking beneath an open sky, responding to its everchanging moods, scents, sounds, temperature and colour. Writings often accompany drawings in my notebooks, recording my reactions to a place as an emotional sensation. When working outdoors I paint and draw copiously, scribbling numerous notations and images. Back in the studio the moment is relived and explored anew, the accumulation of this imagery an important reminder of being in, rather than merely looking at, the landscape. Exhibition catalogues containing poems alongside my paintings can be requested from colinslater@waitrose.com."

SUNRISE

The stilly night was over,
The stars had faded fast,
And there, on the horizon,
Beyond Chelveston mast,
I saw a sight so beautiful,
As gilded banners furled,
The early dawn, just breaking,
And light shed on the world.

I saw the bright sun rising,
And the night cloud, steal away,
I saw the pearly scarves of mist
That along the valley lay;
The ascending lark, exulting,
Sang his song of praise,
The leveret clung to his mother's breast
And the sheep began to graze.

The swallows cried, beyond the stream,
And the flowers rose to the sun,
The dewy grass wept, joyfully,
And the summer had begun.

Margaret Whitworth, Rushden, Northamptonshire

HEAVY BLUES

The notes are black
And heavy
As crawfish
Are pulled wriggling
By gnarled hands
In secret bayous
Modern freight flows
Down a long Mississippi
Past rotting jetties
And rusting machinery
Old boats
Rocking
In the wake

Paul Wilkins, Northampton, Northamptonshire

FUTURAMA

Winter land, sea and sand
Recede with a wave of a magic wand
Snowflakes settle on a beach
Where shells beseech you to ignore the sounds
Of everyday barking hounds
Bounding over breakwaters
Swinging louvre doors
Brown label tea bag for a hag
Round not strong, cheap and wrong

Split the bag and read the leaves
Sheaves of corn on a summer's day
You and me old and grey
Like the waves of the sea on a winter's day
Sleeping and waking every day
In strawberry fields where we shall lay
Writing and reading every day

Mary Ricketts, Wellingborough, Northamptonshire

FREE BIRD

Free bird can I fly beside you
Feel your spirit lifting me higher?
I want to be the eagle, the owl and the dove
The phoenix being born in the fire

You've made me feel both vulnerable and safe
Like no one else has ever done
You'd be the one I'd trust to catch me
If I ever flew too close to the sun

I'm looking forward to whatever time we have
No matter what tomorrow brings
Because I know when I listen to my soul
I'll hear the song that the free bird sings

Jacqui Hancox, Daventry, Northamptonshire

WEDNESDAYS

Set adrift in the middle of the week
Working for five days is like sailing the channel on a lily-pad

It's been two days since I left the shores of last weekend
It will be another two until I see the sandy beach of Friday night

Every minute that passes brings me a minute closer to my destination
I drift with the current

It's all we can do

Andrew Martin, Northampton, Northamptonshire

MY FAITHFUL FRIEND

Here I sit with you by my side
Watching the embers glow
You are always there to cheer me
Even when I'm feeling low
You never even ask for much
Just food and water really
A nice long walk across the fields
Will suit you quite ideally
One day I know we'll have to part
It's a day I surely dread
Because I know it will break my heart
As I sit by your empty bed

Beryl Wetherall, Kettering, Northamptonshire

Born in Kettering **Beryl Wetherall** enjoys cooking, reading and walking. "I started writing poetry in 1999 after my second breakdown," she explained. "My first poem was inspired by watching a young child playing and my work is influenced by people and places. I would describe my style as easy to understand and with a message. I would like to be remembered as someone who is always willing to lend a helping hand." Aged 56 Beryl is a housewife with an ambition to live a long, happy and healthy life. She is married to Gordon and they have one son, Darren. "As well as a short story I have written many poems and had several published," she said.

THE DREAM OF LOVE

Floating on a sigh,
Like a sun-kissed rose petal
Falling to the ground,
The dream of love
Drifts around the mind,
Weaving a fantasy,
A mere whisper
Of a thousand tomorrows.
Stealing over the heart,
Penetrating the depths of the soul,
To lie in wait
For the precious moment when
Love is awakened.

M S Reid, Corby, Northamptonshire

COVERED IN THE COLOUR PURPLE

I curl up in pain in the corner
Of an empty room,
Covered in the colour purple.
I cry and call out,
But nobody hears my suffering.
I'm left alone as usual
To think and reflect
What I have done wrong.
I must say sorry,
I must dress down,
I must stay in the house,
I must be quiet
I must, I must, I must
If I'm obedient
She won't strike me again,
A helpless man,
Until... I do something wrong.

Lorraine Diep, Northampton, Northamptonshire

TOGETHERNESS

Momentarily, we walk and talk
Thoughts joined like cherries on a single stalk.
Enough for pleasure, but without the love,
So it would seem.

Cherries are sweet, sun-ripened to eat,
Their red juice bleeding on our dusty streetwise feet
On hands that join, in love or out,
Sensually supreme.

If you should stand too near
I'd deck you with twin cherries on each ear
Then bite between them, wakening the love
Which could let loose the dream.

Diana Cockrill, Bugbrooke, Northamptonshire

HAIKU

Dreams going cold
Tears running still
Liquid solidify sing

Matthew Williams, Northampton, Northamptonshire

Matthew Williams said: "I have been writing fragments - poems, thoughts, short stories and lyrics for many years. I usually write in the quiet moments, what Simon Armitage dubbed as 'stolen time'. I am working on a poetry collection called 'Muscle' which I hope will be finished in 2002, as well as a short story, 'Apologetica'. Influences on my writing come from everywhere. I am 23 and currently unemployed and my ambition is to write and publish a novel/collection of short stories while still a young writer. I would like to be remembered as someone who knew the weight of words."

FELL TO DIE

Juvenile crow
Lying in the grass
Forgotten
Alone
This peaceful creature
In lifeless sleep
Fell to its sad end
Before it even took flight
Never had a chance
To embrace the open sky
Fell to die
From its nest
To rest
In death's hands
Underbelly feathers
Soft
Not quite bloomed
Flicker in the breeze
This sad moment moves me

John Davies, Kettering, Northamptonshire

I thank life for being my teacher, and my family and friends, who make this life beautiful. Love to all.

HE COUGHED IN THE LIBRARY

The yellow sign on the wall above the reading table whispers
Kindly refrain from making noise for the benefit of others.

A man in a business suit blows dust from a book sleeve.
The noisy expulsion causes a rustle amongst the serious readers
They hate to be disturbed.

I wonder as I step in sneakers round the untouched shelves
Whether under the readers are brighter patches of colour.

Focussed on their pursuit they never look or go outside
Or read a newspaper or go home, the world is the library,
Everything is in books.

Then he coughed in the library, the world turned
Then it muttered at the disturbance and turned back to its book.

But to me the cough was a sound a book couldn't re-create
And I knew the world was outside too
And I went with him, to see the world he knew.

Sarah Jones, Higham Ferrers, Northamptonshire

Sarah Jones said: "I am an 18-year-old student about to start my first year studying English and Theatre in Performance at the University of Plymouth. My hobbies include writing, in a number of genre, reading and amateur dramatics. I began competitively writing poetry after entering an Ottaker and Faber's poetry competition and winning through to the final. I have since then spent a lot of time learning my craft in an effort to gain understanding and skill, and consider 'He Coughed In The Library', my first nationally published piece, both reward for my work and encouragement for the future."

HOLIDAY

As we left the sandy shore,
The sun was setting down beneath the horizon
The sun was like a light bulb,
Surrounded by its own colourful reflection.
The wind is a hand.
Pushing the golden sand into the air,
And letting it go again.
The clear blue sea walked farther and farther away,
As the sun was hidden behind it.
But as soon as the night had fallen,
The clear blue sea would start its journey back.

Katie Li, Northampton, Northamptonshire

SHE REMEMBERS

She remembers the fires, blackouts and bombs.
And the cathedral, its steeples bright,
all aglow on a wintry Midlands night.

She remembers the rations, wardens and WAAFs.
And the Liver Bird, its wings alight,
all aglow on a rainy Mersey night.

She remembers the telegrams, dances and dates.
And the shipping, such a sight,
all aglow on a stormy Atlantic night.

She remembers the wireless, speeches and songs.
And the enemy, smashed by Right,
all aglow on a devastated Dresden night.

But, most of all she remembers.. ellipses him.

Tim French, Northampton, Northamptonshire

FLASH

She was frightened of dark
needed nightlight to unspell the dark
lost certainty when people changed, turning dark

not a child,
no excuse for dark aversion
to the curtained unknown.

Then he was there, strong, reassuring,
and dark.

Sally Angell, Kettering, Northamptonshire

MY BEST FRIEND

His velvet paws,
they make no sound,
but pitter-patter on the ground.

His deep blue eyes twinkle like stars,
and his nose is coloured,
just like Mars.

When he wags his golden tail,
it looks nothing more
but like a sail.

People stop to say hello,
and, my, what a handsome fellow.

Laura Walker, Kingsthorpe, Northampton, Northamptonshire

Dedicated to my grandparents, John and Vivienne, my mum, Jane and my loving pets Chlòe and Maisy.

IF I WERE AN ADULT

If I were an adult
The moon is where I'd go.
I'd travel in my rocket
And look at earth below.

If I were an adult
The Queen is who I'd be.
Waving at my subjects
Wishing they were me.

If I were an adult,
My gran is who I'd see.
I wish she was alive,
To sit me on her knee.

If I were an adult
Clouds are what I'd feel.
See if they were cotton wool
Pretending to be real.

If I were an adult
And could be just right here.
Then I would do all these things
And show no signs of fear.

Sarah Eden, Corby, Northamptonshire

THE DEVIL

The devil didn't love you, the devil didn't care
Now the devil will leave you empty and bare.
The devil causes heartache, the devil causes pain,
The devil will leave you cold on the higher plane.
The devil doesn't listen, the devil only wants,
The devil only tempts to leave you crying out in vain.

Paula Glynn, Towcester, Northamptonshire

FOREVER

Speak your last words,
Let them linger in bodies, minds and souls.
May they be suspended over a pile of sodden soil,
In a grey graveyard with wilting flowers and weeping willows.

Soft air is passing through tender lips,
Whispering goodbye.
The heaving chest collapsing and eyes shutting,
Never to see again.
Witnesses to love, fear and beauty,
But words are what I hear now.
Syllables floating upon clouds,
Falling on deafened ears,
Slicing through silence.

By the time their journey is over you are gone,
The sound ringing in my ears,
The words imprinted on my soul,
Forever.

Juliet Pedersen, Kettering, Northamptonshire

MY GARDEN

My garden I would rather be
it is my place of sanctuary
there is always something different to see
and it always seems to draw me.

Its addictive therapeutic powers
can keep me occupied for hours
each day always something new to see
so many flowers and varieties.

The birds sing merrily in the trees
oh what such creativity
the butterflies, frogs and the bees
what better place could one be?

Cynthia Fay, Maidwell, Northampton, Northamptonshire

I dedicate this poem to Mum and Dad, from whom I learnt my love of gardening. Glory be to God.

COLOURFUL BLOOMS

Colours I like to see
Appear throughout the year

Delicate snowdrops, fresh green and white
Piercing crocus, purple so bright

Cheerful daffodils, yellow and cream
Woodland bluebells, scent is a dream

Fiery tulips, eye-catching red
Smiling pansies, a colourful bed

Delicate spiraea, arches of snow
Climbing clematis, steal the show

Luscious grasses, send green spears
Sad little fuchsias, shed purple tears

English roses, pink, red and peach
Entwined with passion-flower, far out of reach

Busy lizzies, which never tire
Red-hot pokers, in shades of fire

Flat-headed sedums, pink and stout
Creeping ivy, reaching out

Holly berries, cherry red
A new beginning, just ahead

Lynn Neal, Kettering, Northamptonshire

I dedicate 'Colourful Blooms' to my late grandad, Robert Johnston. He first inspired my interest in gardening and flowers. Thank you.

BOB'S PICTURE

Just look at that seascape.
Have you ever seen a picture
Where you could so feel yourself
Right there, on the beach, sand
Between your toes, waves caressing
Your feet?

Look at the clouds. White fluffy in
The blue, almost floating from the frame.
Just relax, sit there and enter in.
A holiday on your wall, waiting
For you, to renew energy and joy
Your mind.

Yes, it is a wonderful painting.
There is atmosphere, peace, tranquillity.
How did he do it? Put in all that love?
Oh, by the way, I don't know if I said
He has a special gift, he paints with
His mouth.

Elizabeth Morris, Kettering, Northamptonshire

TIME

Counting coins
Checking change
Investing shrapnel in the gut
Swirling circles
Increase their speed
Fumbling accountancy count checking twice
Bells toll
Bottles hell
As coins escape the elusive eye
Doubling crowds diminishing finds
Incessant bells toll so bottles fell
Fables and faerie tales of meandering minds

Jennifer Stoole, Corby, Northamptonshire

DARK NEWS

Shadow
Lung
Words meaning nothing
Meaning everything

Mind
Numb
Eyes gaze unseeing
Not believing

Operation
Radiation
Lips acquiescing
Fervently hoping

Something can be done

Jacqueline Sammarco, Northampton, Northamptonshire

MRS MORLEY

Thou shalt go, dear to know
angels, every one
Thou, shalt wonder never more
Wherest goes, the sun

Alighted see, the lilac tree
and breathe it's sweet perfume
Thou shalt wonder never more
Wherest goes the moon

Thou shalt bide, with love beside
and walk the golden way
Thou shalt wonder never more
Wherest goes, the day

For thou art blessed
as none more surely,
Where thou goest,
Mrs Morley

Richard Rochester, Raunds, Northamptonshire

MEMORIES

Memories can be really precious
Memories can be sad
Memories can be sometimes painful
But to have them I am glad
Without them how would we know
That at times it's been so good
To remember things that we have done
That we never thought we could?
So treasure yours forever now
Hold them close to your heart
Remember people and places that you love
And hope they never part.

Shelley Froggatt, Long Eaton, Nottinghamshire

FLOWER

Gently but slowly
The flower uncurls
Showing its beauty
Like thousands of pearls.

The sun shines upon her
With terrible heat
Until the flower
Is stamped on by feet.

No more light in the world
And the world ain't the same
No more beauty to see
And are the feet there to blame?

Elena Uteva, Beeston, Nottinghamshire

ONCE WE WERE YOUNG

Once we were young; but yesterday;
For youth is brief, it slips away
Uncurbed as water in the hand,
Unbridled as the shifting sand,
Its death impossible to stay.

The young believe life's theirs, for they
Such arrogance and scorn display,
We smile, for we both understand,
Once we were young.

But growing old holds no dismay
For joys and mem'ries far outweigh
The fate mortality has planned;
Now clinging to life's final strand
Our thoughts to our first passions stray,
Once we were young.

Hilary Cairns, Retford, Nottinghamshire

LAW IN YOUR OWN HANDS

It's over, the hype, the headlines have gone.
The soldiers gone to fight, the workers gone to work,
The dead laid to rest, the fear not.
Fear of planes, fear of crowds, fear of freedom
Three thousand five hundred died that day, along with,
went millions more.
Not leaving the home alone, avoiding busy streets,
quiet parks should not be a life routine.
I don't mean the obvious alone, but deeper,
not just the families of those stolen, but others also.
Those being punished for those who deserve more than just
punishment. The ignored, the beaten, the bullied,
The murdered.
Those being brought to harm by those who think
They know best, know how to play the law.
All because of those eight.
Who brought harm to a world.
I'm talking about those suffering an injustice undeserving.

Kirsty Timmins, Retford, Nottinghamshire

COMPARING HUMANS WITH THE GOLDEN EAGLE

The golden eagle stands up high,
He glides through the air as the scenes go by.
Gliding through the sky in his normal straight line
Peace and tranquillity is combined
The golden eagle is gathering twigs for its secretive lair.
Our rushing life is nothing to compare.

Adam Collingburn, Retford, Nottinghamshire

OH COME NOW VIOLENT

Oh come now violent
From the broken rocks
And rake with your gales
The embers of the blackening sun;

Come split the seed
And crack the skull;
Roar white below the grey brain
Till it hisses, spits and dances.

Oh come now sudden
Before glass myths
Bloom with the cold
And vision cataracts

While sparrows stab among the crumbs of Eden
And the sleeping chalice burns in her hand.

Arthur Barlow, Long Eaton, Nottinghamshire

A MORNING IN SCOTLAND

Frosty morning cold as ice
Covered white, crisp and nice,
Fingers tingling toes all numb
Flowers waiting for the sun
Trees all frozen in time and space
Cobwebs dangle like fragile lace
Pathways sparkle with diamonds bright
Till they give way to warmth and light

Julia Sell, Mansfield, Nottinghamshire

WHY DO WE?

Why do we laugh
Why do we cry
Why do we let
Our lives pass us by?

Why do we run
Why do we hide
Why is it to strangers
We always confide?

Why are we here
Why do we live
Why do we take
Why do we give?

Why do we love
Why do we hate
Why do we leave
Everything to fate?

Kerry Tasker, Retford, Nottinghamshire

STANLEY SPENCER

And on that morning they shall awaken
to smells of coffee, eggs and bacon.
They will cast off all greyness as their feet touch the floor,
pick up their spirits from the hooks on each door
bleary eyes shuffle to the bathroom of eternal redemption
where they will bathe away all of their earthly tension.
Naked or robed in the spirit divine,
they will leave their homes at the usual time;
but instead of to the factory, office or shop,
they will throng through the streets to the celestial stop.
The bus will be waiting, the driver is on board,
to take them from Cookham to the arms of the Lord.

Stuart Whomsley, Newark, Nottinghamshire

FATE

At the tea dance he made straight for you
Despite fiancé, escort, courtesy.
But without courtesy fate whispered
"Your husband," your master, your lord.

Years later, you wondered if this were
A trick; after the bondage, mastery,
Manipulation, after your two sons.
After work makes free.

Like the two-edged sword,
What defends, cuts; what frees, binds.
Fate laughed his wordless joke.
Then one day, he quietly died.

David Barratt, Farnsfield, Nottinghamshire

Dedicated to Jarmilla Urbanovà, whose life in Prague from World War One to the present mirrors the century's tragedies and triumphs.

FORGOTTEN CHILD

My Lord, I sit and think of her
betrayed, bereft and feared.
For he see did see the life in her,
Her power, wild and weird.

My Lord, I ask you this my friend,
Will you help me find my way?
He took my child, my heart, my life,
And now the world is grey.

We were once so close, the three of us,
a loving, happy three
So I ask you one thing more my Lord
Forgive this man for me.

Elizabeth Baxter, Rainworth, Nottinghamshire

Born in Mansfield **Elizabeth Baxter** is influenced by Tolkien and other fantasy writers. "I have been writing since I was a child," she pointed out. "It is something I have always felt compelled to do and my style is mostly introspective and thoughtful. I would like to be remembered as someone whose writing affected people on an emotional level." Aged 23, she is a banker with an ambition to make a living from full-time writing. "I write fantasy novels and short stories and my biggest fantasy is to win the Nobel Prize for literature. The person I would most like to meet is Terry Pratchett because he is such a successful fantasy writer and I am sure he could give me lots of tips."

TELL HER

Tell her, long after she'd gone
I kept her things
Mention that I hate this distance
Ask her to come back.
Tell her, when she speaks poetry
That's all I can hear
And when she says flowers
That's all I can see.

John Hodges, Newark, Nottinghamshire

FRAGRANT BUTTERFLY

I have noted your disapproval and will now cease to pursue
I have no regrets of the past or present and the thoughts I held for you
I guess I am all the richer for whatever it was we found
For me perhaps a pool of affection in which I duly drowned
Time passes us by so quickly
With anxieties every single day
We work so hard and laugh so little
But our offspring continue to play
Now I have time to read and write plus endless hours of thought
Concealed in my heart memories of cherished times and the smiles you so easily brought
Was it a source of amusement a type of trivial pursuit?
Or maybe somewhere there was warmth and emotions you readily sought to recruit
You were eager of the offer of pleasures of the flesh and accepted them just as I
I am so sorry you chose to clip the wings of this fragrant butterfly

Valerie Morgan, Retford, Nottinghamshire

JOY

To melt mind
in art-crucible

to form a soul-creative
thus a soul of joy;

as contrasts and contradictions
resolve in paint and prose;

as colours and consonants
fill the disemvowelled canvas.

John Hopkins, Newark, Nottinghamshire

MY DIET

I realised the other day,
that I was getting fat,
So I sat down and pondered
what I could do about that.
It seemed my only option
was to cut down on my food,
The only problem was
it all tastes so good.

Oh isn't there anything
to help me in my plight,
Anything at all that will
help me win the fight?
I wondered and wondered
just what it would take
Then went out and
bought myself
A great big chocolate cake.

Pat Rogers, Cotgrave, Nottinghamshire

CREATIVE DRINKING

Now what do you mean by creative?
Ah, there's the rub.
Can you do the creative work anywhere?
Or must it be in a pub?

Some people become very eloquent
After a few pints of ale.
Some whistle and sing, some don't do a thing
But just sit there looking pale.

Some people become most aggressive
And want to start a brawl
And others become quite possessive
And that doesn't do, not at all.

But some, now they're really creative
Their minds become clear as a bell,
Their genius erupts when they're well in their cups
They can work out maths problems as well.

And produce some wonderful paintings
Others wonderful music compose
When heady with wine, poets think they're divine
And produce real poetry, not prose.

Pamela Field, Southwell, Nottinghamshire

LONELY BIRD'S DREAMS

We're travelling around time,
Searching for a reason to believe in.
Trying to forget the dark
and find the sunshine inside us.

Whispering for a broken silence
Empty dream, lonely bird's birth.

My tears are always there,
in my thoughts in my dreams.
In your eyes.

I'm watching you in the sunset,
and I discover another world in your smile.

Shadow in the wind.
The wind is a shadow of your soul,
who brings to my heart
every star of the universe.

Dreaming for a broken silence.
Lonely dream.
Lonely bird's death.

Alan McLane, Beeston, Nottinghamshire

RETIRING THOUGHTS

In all the things you've worked for
And accomplished in the past,
May you take some satisfaction
And find memories which last.

In all the things you've hoped for
And in all you plan to do
May a very special happiness
Be waiting there for you.

No need to watch the ticking clock
You'll have no need of time
For now's the time you've worked for
And you now are in your prime.

Ian Gray, Wollaton Park, Nottinghamshire

RACISM

If I was black would you hurt me?
If I was black could you see?
If I was a different shade of colour,
I'd still be myself, just me.

An Asian lies in the street,
Bruised, hurt, beat,
Would you go over and help him?
The chances of that would be quite slim.
You think most people aren't racist,
Well racism does exist.

Does it really matter about the colour of your face,
If you think about it,
We're all the same race.

Corey Martin, Newark, Nottinghamshire

NUMERACY

No man is an island, or so the sages say
We were not meant to be alone forever and a day.
We all need company to share our happiness or strife
And spend our time searching for a husband or a wife.

For two can pull together working as a pair,
Like birds and beasts, we also need somebody to share.
Then from two, a third appears a child for both to love
To complete the little family sent from God above.

Our lives are ruled by numbers, as we live from day to day,
Notice how it affects our actions in every kind of way.
Numeracy is everywhere in the Bible it is true
Adam and Eve and their two sons to name but a few.

Some say God does not exist, so tell me if you can
If not God, who designed this miracle of man
Someone created the fish beneath the sea
Plus the moon and stars, so why not little me?

Hazel Walters, Trowell, Nottinghamshire

Hazel Walters said: "I have been writing poetry seriously since 1992 and I have had work published in seven anthologies plus many times in the four local newspapers. I get my inspiration out of the blue, usually the first line as I wake up in the morning. Then before I can do anything else, I have to get the bones of it down on paper. Many of my poems start out as an exercise at my writing club, (The Trowell and District Writers' Trust) as did this one. I have been married to Arthur for 48 years and we have three children. My hobbies, besides poetry and story writing, are cross-stitch, crosswords, painting and watching soap operas."

FLASHBACK

A mass of copper curls, eyes smiling
Wide and blue under fluttering, dark lashes.
Full lips lined in scarlet.
Beautiful.

First kiss, soft like a feather,
Slow and sweet.
Never want to let her go.
Beautiful.

Reds and golds of a Spanish sunrise,
And the pinks, purples and blues of the sunset
And your fireworks that night.
Beautiful.

Promise of love forever,
In a glistening diamond ring.
Beautiful.

She wanted carnations and lilies
The flowers shimmer in the sunshine
Shining with sad tears
A last kiss goodbye
Beautiful.

Lisa Sapey, East Bridgford, Nottinghamshire

WHERE IS YESTERDAY?

Where is yesterday?
No one can really say
It used to be tomorrow
I watched a day slowly go
It soon became today
But a day will never stay
Soon it will be long ago
What is it that's making the time flow?
Our time is slowly running out
Just what's it all about?
Our lives are much too short
I wish I'd never had this thought
Or started this poem

Charles Baker, Retford, Nottinghamshire

CRUCIBLE

High clouds
move with fine music
in this sky I love,
its air fresh and strange,
its light playful and shimmering,
a veil for my doubts.
The new day trembles
between sunshine and rain
like my faith
Taking the early morning light,
blending it
with longings for peace and grace,
I shall celebrate
when the dove spreads its wings.

Peter Day, Newark, Nottinghamshire

LUNACY

I say that I love her forever more,
But I don't expect her to answer me,
I see her shimmering along the shore,
Reflected in the calmness of the sea.
She attracts water, including the seas.
And may be ancient but looks quite youthful,
And though some say that she is made of cheese,
She will remain forever beautiful.
Her magical gaze is an enigma,
For in the night, she is the enchantress,
In Roman times, she was called Diana,
It's no wonder that she was a goddess.
So next time she shines, and you stand and stare
If people say that you're mad, just don't care.

John Oxley, Selston, Nottinghamshire

Born in Uttoxeter **John Oxley** enjoys cycling, music, drawing, poetry and helping in his children's activities. "I only started writing poetry recently," he remarked. "I was inspired by my recent studies in English Literature and my work is influenced by Wordsworth, Shakespeare and nature. I would describe my style as pantheistic and I would like to be remembered for expressing my love and concern for the natural environment through my poetry." Aged 36, John is a community care assistant for Nottinghamshire County Council Social Services. He is studying for a law degree and hopes to join the legal profession. He is married to Louise and they have two daughters, Alexandra and Gabriella.

PUMPKIN

Maybe I am mistaken.
It is midnight and I am standing
on the balcony wearing both glass slippers
I have tried throwing myself at a dozen spinning wheels
and choking on these poisoned apples,
I am confused
My Prince Charming speaks to me only to confide about his
new Snow White and all the wrong Romeos call up to me
Should I let down my hair?
Is this a fairy-tale?
Perhaps I am reading it upside down,
Or inside out.

Frances Bowman, Mansfield, Nottinghamshire

EINSTEIN

Einstein
His brain was fine
Inventing all his life
Now he's vapourised his wife

Einstein
His brain was fine
Inventing for all he's worth
Now he's been blasted off this earth

Professor Einstein was so fine
He had the best way to dine
First the food appears
And then the drink comes out his ears

Jamie Lee, Eastwood, Nottinghamshire

WAR

War is not something we should remember or glorify
Wives waving husbands and sons off to be maimed or die
We must think positive and make sure it doesn't happen again
The hurt and destruction is just insane
The slogan Your Country Needs You was perfectly right
To build a better world to live in not to fight
Remember the people that were not there by choice
Those brave troops that had no voice
Lest we should forget let's hope and pray
We never have to celebrate another VE Day.

L Hunt, Retford, Nottinghamshire

THE LITTLE DOG LAUGHED

The moon raced across the sky
a mad March hare,
jumping over jets,
out-sprinting the stars
in the silvery light;
the hills illuminated
as stage scenery.
Windows rattled,
doors slammed,
gusts ripped the children's pictures
off the walls.
Our dog barked
as strangers toppled tiles.
I fancied my beard
blown sideways
as if drawn by Lear;
and the dish blew
away with the spoon.

Derek Hughes, Newark, Nottinghamshire

THE PERFECT SUNDAY

Lean roast beef, a Yorkshire pud,
onion gravy, roasted spud,
cabbage white and Brussels sprout,
piping hot to keep cold out.

Juicy carrots, garden peas,
cauliflower as big as trees,
sometimes sweetcorn, sometimes swedes,
grown by me from packet seeds.

To top it all there's tateys mashed.
I'll scoff the lot quite unabashed.
And when I've eaten food so good,
I'll wait awhile before the pud.

Treacle tart or spotted dick,
but not enough to make you sick,
with bags of custard made with milk,
slips down a treat, like creamy silk.

And after that a can of booze
and then perhaps a little snooze,
with mouth wide open, snoring free,
dreaming of my coming tea.

George Miles, Walkeringham, Nottinghamshire

VODKA BREATHING

Vodka breathing
Drunken Sundays
Slow smoke curling
From languid cigarettes
Fingers tracing
Erotic pulse beats
Amidst vodka hilarity
Long kisses
Orange-tasting sunshine
Room, people
Turning, falling, spinning
Vodka breathing

Helen Ambler, Whitwell, Worksop, Nottinghamshire

MAYBE

The winds of change blow ever near
Can't take away this taste of fear
Storms are brewing in my mind
Maybe calm will follow and fate will be kind
Or maybe my life will turn upside down
My anxious smiles will become a frown
The eternal flame of hope burnt out
With an everlasting shower of disappointment and doubt
Or maybe happiness will step right in
Take away the shadows of the night
That crawl around in my brain until daylight
My lust for life will reappear, and drive away that lonely tear
Hope will never fade as long as I am alive
For a better life I will continue to strive
Maybe this, maybe that
Who knows what will happen to me
I'll just make a wish, cross my fingers, then wait and see.

Heather McKie, Hucknall, Nottinghamshire

ONLY ONE IN LOVE

They say fools rush in
And it never was more true
Than on that April morning
The day that I met you

The film star looks
The dazzling smile
First place, won the race
I'd beaten everyone else by a mile

Like a lamb to the slaughter you led me
To what I thought would be new highs
How was I to know for you
It was just a pack of lies?

Everyone told me it was coming
They said it was at an end
But I just kept on believing
The last one to pretend

Why do I always do this?
The first one whose hopes rise to skies above
And the very last to realise
I'm the only one in love

Howard Hunt, Carlton, Nottingham, Nottinghamshire

SHE'S SEVEN, GOING ON TWENTY

She's seven going on twenty
My darling little daughter.
The words that she comes out with
Can fill the house with laughter
On a good day.

I find it most frustrating
When she's getting dressed for school,
That in June we still wear trousers
Red and white checked dresses aren't cool
It's summer uniform.

She goes to dance and drama
For which we have to pay
To learn techniques, gain confidence
"She lacks this not," I say

She's not like me when I was small
I often did as I was told,
They grow up so fast, they're barely kids
A sure sign I'm getting old.
Like policemen looking younger.

Rosemary Rowe, Forest Town, Mansfield, Nottinghamshire

MIGRAINE BLUES

Dark cloud, dark cloud, oh, what a thief,
You steal my joy and give me grief;
I just can't tell where you're coming from,
But I can't stand it when you're coming on strong.

Dark cloud, dark cloud, you fog my mind,
You make me feel so undefined,
You trouble my thoughts, I can't concentrate,
For you have the power to disorientate.

Dark cloud, dark cloud, you haunt my soul,
Stirring the depths, swirling out of control:
I aim to resist you dragging me down,
But you still turn my smile to a frown.

Dark cloud, dark cloud, you are bad news,
But I'll be free from the migraine blues:
You'll never win and you'll never hide,
When peace flows through from heaven's side.

There was a time, you had to flee,
When Jesus calmed the Sea of Galilee:
Beware as you thunder along my shore,
For the Son will banish you forevermore.

Nicholas Whitehead, Newark, Nottinghamshire

SURFING

Imagine time as an ocean,
With now the wave-crest you ride.
Fate, life's direction and motion,
Let this be the incoming tide.
The beach called death lies before you.
At your heels flies the spume of your past.
Heed the moment, my friend, I implore you,
And live it as if it's your last.

George Shipley, Mansfield Woodhouse, Nottinghamshire

FIREWORKS

On November nights they light the sky
Brilliant colours exploding in the air
Jumping jacks, crackling, whizzing
Catherine wheels on the fences fizzing
Roman candles send up golden plumes,
Sparklers twirling in the gloom
Jacket potatoes, hot dogs too
Bonfire toffee, tea, coffee, you can choose
Dogs cower in the house shivering and shaking
Barking, growling, can't stop quivering

On the bonfire sits the guy aloft
Rockets for ears, Catherine wheels for eyes
Garbed in old coat, shoes, hat and mask
To make him was the children's task
The bonfire's lit, crackles and blazes
See the joy reflected on people's faces
Smoke-filled eyes, cold feet, tingling fingers
Round the fire we all still linger
While acrid smoke fill the air and floats
In drifts across the neighbours' gardens

Vera Bailey, Newark, Nottinghamshire

SUMMER NOISE

Out in the garden here today
sounds of summer come out to play.
Lawns being cut, what a lovely smell
sending snails into their shells.

Neighbours laughing, sharing jokes
talking together these village folks.
Cars with windows open wide
from one end of the road to the other side.

Birds are singing, taking baths
the postman up and down our paths
making time to say hello
letter boxes to and fro
cards and gifts landing on the mat
barely missing our pet cat.

Deck-chairs and recliners all set out
can you hear a distant shout?
Workmen on their way down the hill
Oh no, they are coming with their drill.
Summer noise is mostly sweet
but not when they dig up our street.

Julie Mawman, Newark, Nottinghamshire

TAKING EARLY RETIREMENT

Take early retirement dear, you're almost fifty-six
Take early retirement dear, you're getting in a fix
You really have seen better days, you're past your sell-by date,
Take early retirement dear, you cannot afford to wait.

I listened to their good advice, decided to take a chance
Lots of free time to travel, to read good books or to dance
To visit old acquaintances to learn some things that are new
Each day so full of promise, so many things to do.

Then suddenly it happened, it all came into view
I'll become an adult learner. Yes, that's what I will do.
I'll go and learn computing and how to surf the net
Did you think I was finished, I haven't started yet.

I really do like learning, although it takes some time
To get each skill implanted into this brain of mine
Learning about the keyboard and how to use the mouse
I never thought the day would come when I'd have one in the house.

So the moral of this story is, it never is too late,
To have a go with learning,
Don't be past your sell-by date.

Maureen Hames, Retford, Nottinghamshire

THE WOLF AND THE TODDLER

Once upon a time there was a wolf
Who lived in the Forest of Gulf
This wolf was very nice
But he always mistook children for rice

But one day this all changed
When a toddler walked through in the rain
He found the wolf lying on its back
Eating a cheesy flavour bag of NikNaks

The toddler knew about the wolf
Who lived in the Forest of Gulf
He said, "Please, Mr Wolf, don't eat me.
I'm not tasty as you can see.

"The thing that's more tasty than me,
Is rice as most of us can see.
A way to know which is which, as most children fear,
Is that children have longer ears."

Jack Sadler, Worksop, Nottinghamshire

THOUGHTS UNSAID

I hear you in my head,
See you in my mind,
I feel you in my heart,
But for one day only,
I wish I could feel your touch,
Feel your soft warm skin,
All your tenderness and love,
Flowing from within.

If only I could steal
Just one more day,
One more hour,
To tell you how much I loved you,
How much I want to share,
If only I'd thought,
If only I'd said,
If only I'd shown,
Now there's no time left,
Just a lot of if onlys
Roaming my head.

Ann Carratt, Worksop, Nottinghamshire

MY MOON

In twilight I walked
The darkened path
The secrets own
The final pass
To feel nature
On a chilling night
Stars are the lonely light
But where is my moon
In the clear sky?
Remember the reason
Reality lies

Michelle Wragg, Langley Mill, Nottinghamshire

X

I have considered stepping out each night
To muster poems from absence of light,
But my mind is yanked from those thoughts I own
By dew-decked downland in mornings bright.

For my head is like a chariot of bone,
Chasing two horses, whose course is unknown;
And if naught were easy for me to be,
I would slash the straps and step out alone.

But I bite their bit, the reins bent round me,
Choking and chafing, my throat must agree,
One blithe but blundering with all life's zest,
Then the dark, chilled chagrin that I must flee.

I must be, but being, accept the test
That they squeeze tightest when I feel the best.
And often I wish the horses would rest,
And often I wish the horses would rest.

Jonathan Sweet, Nottingham, Nottinghamshire

LOVE UNDER CONSTRUCTION

If I grow old,
Then how old might I be
Before the key
Is turned upon your smile?
When stars swim cold
As fish, arthritic frost
Traces a snail's path
Round my limbs,
Shall I be able to recall
The instant that our covenant
Took shape, in fusty
Sagging beds of rented rooms?
Was it precisely as the pigeon
Crooned in dark-leafed
Sanctuary above our heads
I felt the prospect
Of my future mount,
Promise on promise,
Like an infant's bricks
The cautious process
Of love under construction.

Elizabeth Roff, Oakham, Rutland

A BOUQUET OF LOVE

A little touch of satin, a little touch of lace
With just a touch of silkiness to put it all in place
A tiny sprig of blossom, a little colour blue
A heart so full of happiness is all I wish for you.

A token full of wishes, a basket full of dreams
A gentle cape of tenderness, with love stitched in the seams
A coffer full of memories, a barrel full of pride
A treasure chest of promises to you the groom and bride.

A cosy touch of comfort, and not too many tears
I send you all these blessings as you live your golden years.

Hilary Malone, Oakham, Rutland

HAPPY DAY

His face glowed with glad excitement
Twinkling eyes and smiling lips
"It's a little lad," he hollered
"Worth all those many many trips
To and fro to big consultants
Up and down the London line."

My heart leapt to hear his triumph
My mind raced back forty years
To the very same excitement
Heady mix of laughs and tears
When another young man bellowed
"It's a girl, let's tell the world."

Kirsty Adlard, Newark, Nottinghamshire

THE TRIPPERS

Why do they love only when the weather is fair?
When all the dales' jewelled falls
Sparkle in the sunlight, and hillside woods are fully robed,
And where,
There is no quiet?

Why must you see the countryside all coloured gay
In pleasant mood and smiling sweet?
Queuing for miles on busy roads
To see each beauty spot, to compete
With one another.

Why ceaseless ride to congregate as penned sheep
On each treasured plot of wayside road,
Tied by an invisible umbilical cord
And keep, no
Country Code?

Why not stay and see the dark stark beauty of the moor?
Now hear the winter fullness of the stream
And feel the red cheek stinging of the rain,
And pour out thanks
To God.

Douglas Webb, Mansfield, Nottinghamshire

YOU DO NOT HAVE THE POWER

I do not have the power to judge anyone
I do not have the power to laugh or make fun
But, I do have the power to heal and protect
I do have the power to erase and correct.

If you want me to join you
In your bullying ways
I know I won't accept
As my dad always says.

"Treat people how you would like to be treated yourself
Don't you go picking on anyone else.
It's not right, it's wrong listen to what you heart says
If you do, then you will be guided through the rest of your days."

You do not have the power to judge anyone
You do not have the power to laugh or make fun
As I know you have the power to heal and protect
So go out, be proud
Erase and correct.

Tracey-Louise Bone, Shirebrook, Nottinghamshire

THE MILL

Oh I went up to the mill and I hammered on the door
And the miller shoved his head out, so I asked him, Mister Miller,
What goes on inside your mill?

And he said:-

Oh the sails they turn the windshaft
and the windshaft turns the brakewheel
and the brakewheel turns the wallower
and the wallower turns the crownwheel
and the crownwheel turns the nuts
that spin the stones that grind the grain
to make the meal
to bake the bread

So I watched the flailing arms and I muttered to myself,

Oh the nutcase turns the crankshaft
And the Wallaby turns the windbrake

Or something like that.

John Tait, Sutton-in-Ashfield, Nottinghamshire

SUBVERSIVE

Your subversive, submissions lost faith in the late night
percussions of the blind
where the softness of the world is worn down to the hard-
ness of bone
it broke your bleeding heart
to see it all
how much can you feel?
how much can you hurt?
more than I? or much more than I?
although I left you broken
a fractured man, in a shattered world
the wounds you made in me
have never healed
the blood inside me soiled
with the tired pulsing of a dying life
extinguished by you admission
your pursuit of percussion
late at night, and bled blind

Stanley Chambers, Broughton, Northamptonshire

A SPLENDID PICTURE

We have memories many tucked away in each mind,
Some seem vivid as yesterday some elusive to find,
It is said one stores everything that you never forgot,
All the sunshine and flowers every laugh or regret.

In a span long as this one might wonder quite how,
One could depict events from each birth until now,
And purpose for holding all life's every frame,
Surely one can't extract it and play it again.

So I guess they go with us when at last we depart
Paint a huge splendid picture made of each separate part,
When the final piece forms this vast intricate whole
Perhaps hung up by God and then viewed by us all.

Gary Catlin, Kettering, Northamptonshire

TOWPATH

Open wide fenland skies
Shedding autumn leaves
Dance delirious in a gale
Mocked by naked trees.

Upstream from the low locks
A good two miles or so,
Naming flowers, plants, self
As I slowly go.

Honesty, forsythia,
Ginger-haired loon
Heading for the high locks
In the afternoon.

Lisa Wallace, Stamford, Lincolnshire

THE CHAIR

He sits
open-minded,
expectant
yet resting,
waiting,
his arms
to embrace
and hold,
creaking
back and fore
back and fore
with the age of man,
bearing
and breaking a silence
that forever
protests an innocence of thought

And so they wait
And keep their faith,
their strength,
the man, the boy,
the place that rocks
and gently, safely,
keeps the counsel of time.

Julian Cunnington, Boston, Lincolnshire

NOTHING

Stand around reading, reading all these articles
Articles about writing, writing about anything
But when you want to really get down to it
You can't
You can't seem to pen anything down, type anything down
Anything down
So what do you do?
You write about what you can't seem to do
Funny isn't it, how things turn around
Funny isn't it, how you think too much then come up with something simple
So simple, wonder how I should end it now?

Simran Panaech, Loughborough, Leicestershire

TIME

Tick tock
the sound of the clock
tock tick
the sound of time passing
dusk to dawn
dawn to dusk
where does time go?
where does time stay?
we pray for enlightenment
we pray for that day
tick tock
where does time stay?
tock tick
where does time go?
tick tock
will we ever know?

Kirstin Ferry, Hinckley, Leicestershire

THE SUN

We faced the world, you and I
Never told a promised lie.
We walked in the rain and the moonlit sky,
We name the stars.
Together we saw the sun.

We were united, you and me
I was the land and you the sea.
We surfed your waves and walked my fields,
We made our dreams.
Together we watched the sun.

We need each other, me and you
How else could me make it through?
I was left you were right
Uniting our love to make daylight.
We made our life but caused our death,
Alone I remember the sun.

Rosanna Murphy, Loughborough, Leicestershire

I FEEL IN BETWEEN

As I look towards the golden fields
gracefully swaying to and fro,
I look up at the sky
to see the warm rays of light
which engulf me with a sense of woe.

To feel the wind blowing me with
Its fine, soft breath
and its welcoming coolness in this
summer heat I feel in between
in return a sweet sigh I shall give.

Elizabeth Draycott, Sleaford, Lincolnshire

CLARITY

Steady, rhythmic, silent,
A feathered seeker wanders
From the midst of a dewdrop.
Eyes, full of clarity, full of life.

Ancient memories look on,
Feeling, experiencing
The tingling of harsh reality.

Without fear.
Without dread,
Clarity is lost,
But life remains.

Ripping, tearing, bloody,
Rippling through the undercurrent,
As a moment of innocence ends,
And, once again, a seeker wanders.

Alan Smith, Melton Mowbray, Leicestershire

FIRST LOVE

First love Virginia
I met at Farney Close School
Magic-making in the woods
Loving like young fools.

Brand-new headmaster
Makes woods out of bounds
No magic-making, just hand-holding
Within the school grounds.

First love never forgot
Even twenty years ago
It will last eternally
Till to the Lord's paradise we go.

H G Griffiths, Market Harborough, Leicestershire

MY DAUGHTER VICKI

Our Vicki loved her wellies.
They were pretty shiny and red
She wore them in the sunshine
And when she went to bed

She had a favourite jumper too
It was yellow, red, green and blue
And when she had her hair washed,
She wore her jumper and wellies too
When we wanted to get her jumper to wash
She screamed and hid under the bed
So we washed her jumper
While she was in the bath
And in her wellies all shiny and red

Margaret Shortt, Loughborough, Leicestershire

THE BODY PARTS

I like men with big noses, have you seen Jeff's?
It's like a ski jump - a slammer
Which would have daunted Franz Klammer
In Lillehammer.

His nostrils are flaring, cavernous and proud
As a racehorse tearing along Epsom Downs.

Get a load of his biceps, they ripple and flex,
His six-pack is flat - and along his back
I count cervical one to coccyx thirty-three
Which I can barely see
Over his posing pouch.
Ouch.

His obicularis oris muscles and labial glands
Support a sexy smile and I'd run a mile
To be pressed to his chest; the best, since Arnie's.

His patellas are perky, his quadriceps quirky,
His pelvis is plunging, his loins are lunging.
His flexors are flying and it's no use denying,
Over Jeff I'm a boaster. What a pity he's merely
A pin-up poster.

Norah Hill, Broughton Astley, Leicestershire

ON UNION

The other universal one
The demi-urge
And mystic one
Who put the planets in the sky
And made the world to turn,
The standing stones to glint with sun
The promised son, the golden land
Has all become as one.

What can I say?
The first to smile
The first to laugh
The first to be my other half
To bring me freedom, bring me birth
And be my lawful wedded wife
Who's always there by day and night.

The ripening fruit where rivers run,
The many roads that turn to one,
The standing stones that glint with sun
The ceremony has now begun.

Peter Simon, Padfield, Glossop, Derbyshire

YOU

Your hand is rough with work.
Will you walk with me?

I see dreams in your eyes
And nightmares.
Shall I take your arm?

Your hair is precious
In my sight.
Will we sit together?

I have put you in my soul
For safe keeping
You understand.
And I have seen our love
Reflected perfect
In a peat pool
High on the moor
Just beyond the heather
Next to God.

Maggie Burnside, Matlock, Derbyshire

DIARY

Keep it locked, keep it safe,
no one must see these marks that I make.

The character that I've become
the thoughts that fuel the things I've done.

A girl disloyal, a friend the same,
the way I play the cheating game.

Passionate nights, silent days,
a girl so changed in many ways.

Now he has my smile, he has my kiss,
but my boyfriend, he thinks they're his.

How can it be wrong, we fit like hand in glove,
I've seen the sign I am in love.

I love him in mind, I love him in body,
24 seven, he's becoming my hobby.

Emma Partridge, Chesterfield, Derbyshire

MERCURY MOOD

Let the cutlass of guilt
slice your conscience,
bleed truth,
the gash as deep as lifelong secrets
the pressure of self-pity applied,
drown in your new red fear
infect the wound with hope,
just breathe.
Shed your mental garments
hone your naked nerves
resuscitate your soul,
awake to freedom.

Stephen Hoo, Leicester, Leicestershire

THE GLANCE OF DOOM

I glanced at you across the room.
And my inner fires consume
Then I began to start the chase,
In a silent deadly race,
Which will be my lasting tomb.

Your dark hair shadows my doom.
A desperate life of quiet gloom;
Remembering joy upon my face
Because I glanced.

My pattern woven on a loom,
Laying gutted within my room,
Out of time and out of place
Born to die without a trace;
As the fires of agony consume
Because I glanced.

Stephen Harris, Chesterfield, Derbyshire

COMA

She lay there
Still, motionless
Her life flashed before her eyes
She's not dead
In a coma she lies
Her parents never leave her side
They hold her hand
And tell her tales
Her eyes open
She is awake
Her parents hug
But they're too late
Again she lies
In a coma
Not awake.

Clare Ambrose, Wirksworth, Derbyshire

QUIET MOMENTS

To walk down a lane away from the crowds
Hear the birds singing above in the trees,
Smell the hay in the meadow, know yourself proud
To be part of the countryside, the flowers the bees:
To sit on a stile and drink in the balm
Of quietness, stillness, peace and calm.

Forgetting the stress of the business of life,
Just for brief while all cares depart.
Contentedly losing oneself away from strife
Renewing your spirit and your weary heart.
Seeking refreshment in the soft evening hour.
Mind, heart and soul at peace in the green bower.

Lois Burton, Ilkeston, Derbyshire

CHILDHOOD MEMORIES

Childhood memories of the sweetest kind,
often appear within my mind
I think of all the things I've done and how I always had so much fun.
The long hot summers seemed to pass so slow
and sometimes you'd wonder where to go.
There were holidays outings and days at the park
Where we'd play for hours right up until dark.
Not a care in the world did we have back then,
We just longed for tomorrow to do it all again.
Believing in Santa was a special thing.
Mum and dad knew the joy that would bring.
Christmas Eve up the stairs they would creep hoping to find us fast asleep.
Next to our beds they placed our toys expertly never making a noise.
Seeing our faces thinking Santa had been the excitement in us was a sight to be seen.
So I look back with pleasure at being a kid, remembering every single thing I did.

B Conway, Cleethorpes, Lincolnshire

WE ARE ONE

All my life I have waited for you
In my dreams I saw you
I had kissed you before our lips had ever touched
I held you before our arms were ever entwined
And I had loved you before the warmth of your skin had ever felt mine.
In my eyes I had seen what you had seen.
In my mouth I had tasted what you had tasted.
And in my heart I had felt what you had felt
My mind was your mind.
My body was your body
And my soul is your soul
And now there is no more waiting for you are here
We are one.

Barbara Finlayson, Stoney Middleton, Derbyshire

FOR THE ONE WHO IS LEFT

The sun is a swift beam of yellow
That twinkles and dances in the air
Sprinkling the faces of people with gold
As they wait to greet us, there
Shining on crimsons, gold, greens, and blues
On stained glass reflected on floor
Recalling for me the promises made
A shower of vows are you sure?
Now the flowers, like jewels, are glistening
As they shine through the blur of my tears
Their stems, emerald embers are blistering,
Stretched, like the long-promised years
And the gold band that shines on my finger
Echoes bright memories, aglow in my heart
As I hear you once more say those beautiful words
"To love until death us do part"

Sheila Sharpe, Kegworth, Derbyshire

SEASONS OF LOVE

Oh what a beautiful summer,
Which sadly must come to an end.
But drawn as we are like bees to the flower,
Forever we will remain friends.

With the fall of autumn we watch the leaves,
As they court and dance with the breeze.
Like them we will run with the wind in our hair,
For through life we'll be dancing with ease.

And the coldest darkest winter night,
Can be warmed by the home fires bright.
And my heart will never feel the cold of the snow
While I'm blessed with your love all aglow.

And as the spring thaws the coldest frost,
We know that all's not lost.
For all the new life that does abound.
Just reaffirms the love that we found.

John Antcliffe, Scunthorpe, Lincolnshire

PEACE AND LOVE

What the world needs now
Is peace and love
Mankind united in harmony
No more grief, no more aid or AIDS
The awareness of peace and love
Uniting the world
One heart at a time
So that all can live in peace
Paradise on earth
Is that too much to ask?
You decide for me

Melfyn Dean, Grimsby, Lincolnshire

HOLIDAY VIEW

"This is to be your room," she said,
Flinging wide the shutters on a view
Which lifted my tired spirit like a charm.
In the far distance lay a sea so blue
It seemed unreal, while nearer hills
Rose gently up in varied shades of green.

Tall aloes spiked the air,
And flowers I'd never seen
Splashed purple, white and pink down granite walls.
Just outside the window, from a wooden ledge,
Geraniums crept and looped and trailed
To frame the picture with a blazing edge.

When I was about to turn away,
A pure black cat, compact and neat,
Strolled to the terrace and sat still,
As if to make the scene complete.

Mary Hubble, Grantham, Lincolnshire

SERENITY

Sleep safely, while I whisper in your ear.
Sleep softly, knowing I am near.
As I feel and touch.
Know, I love you very much.
Breath my air, where e'er you be.
See my image,
I have given up to thee.
As I wait my heart is filled.
My life to you, I have now spilled.
Go delicately, gently, harbour me.
For all my life, I will be,
Forever your serenity.

S Sweet, Grimsby, Lincolnshire

APHASIA

Disguised inhibitions
Reluctant meditations
Aphonia
Figuline emotions
Convariant art forms
Entropy
Hedonic depression
Maladroit existence
Phiz
Precipitous leaning
Whimsical feelings
Obruncate
Apodictic prognosis
Decasualize writing
Cachexia

P Lipkowitz, Grimsby, Lincolnshire

THAT'S US

How fragile the humans -
the rash on the face of the earth
who would put the cosmos to rights
with squiggles on paper.
Who would build mighty engines
and talk to the stars.

But what would they say?
Help?

Or
We are the champions.

Leslie Williamson, Eastwood, Nottinghamshire

A LIFE INCOMPLETE

I have a dad who just doesn't care
When friends say they hate their dads
I want to shout; at least he's there

I find my life too hard to handle
Without my dad around, my life feels incomplete
Like the light without the candle

I know I have a terrific mum
Who tries to make up for dad
Not being there, she's also a wonderful friend
Life without her, I couldn't bear

Next to this, I have friends who are there
And unlike my dad
They show that they care

Karen Precious, Rushden, Northamptonshire

CORROSION

I'm 90% sure that when I was about the age of four I knew
all this was all bullshit.

As the glorious blue skies roll by the trivial ants conspire to
despise.

Engrossed in a cabal of copulation to ejaculation to further
what?

Population explosion? give me extreme divination.
A plague on all your houses, a shower of locusts.

Blood flowing in rivers to send shivers.
To move, to move, to move.

C Beniston, Carlton, Nottinghamshire

JENNIFER BREAM

I used to envy Jennifer Bream
her long red hair and skin like cream,
her eyes that sparkled like emeralds fine
I used to wish these things were mine.
But you wanted a girl with cheeks like a rose
and freckles across the bridge of her nose,
with glossy brown hair and dark chocolate eyes.
You wanted me to my surprise.
So now I don't envy Jennifer Bream,
her near-perfect looks are no longer my dream.
Because Jennifer Bream doesn't have you
but I do.

Kathleen Thorpe, Long Eaton, Nottinghamshire

THE DARK HEART'S WISH

I can see your soul on your cheeks
And your spirit in the crease on your brow,
And I've been thinking that
I was meant to meet you somehow,
The reflection in your eyes
Being the image of the man
Who speaks from the shadows
Then takes you by the hand,
Our dreams dance and caress with love
And share in things unplanned
We should yield to the spell
Delivered from this wand.

Stephen Fletcher, Keyworth, Nottinghamshire

BLOSSOM TIME

A special time, a special season.
Magnificent grandeur of blossom reborn.
It's magical. Mystical God is the reason;
For creating such loveliness to greet each morn.
Hawthorn adorns meadows in May.
Kissed by the morning dew.
Where there were dead leaves, and decay
Earth comes alive again. Everything's new.
Boulevards lined with cherry trees
Candy-pink petals, perfect in shape.
Precise in timing. Never late.
Buzzing about are busy bees.
As the season passes, and time has flown
Each petal falls graciously. Silently blown.
"Do not be grieved for us" they said.
"We're only asleep. We are not dead."

Elizabeth Bigg, Long Eaton, Nottinghamshire